America's Prisons

America's Prisons

The Movement Toward Profit and Privatization

Curtis R. Blakely

BrownWalker Press
Boca Raton, Florida USA
2005

America's Prisons:
The Movement Toward Profit and Privatization

Copyright © 2005 Curt R. Blakely

BrownWalker Press
Boca Raton , Florida
USA • 2005

ISBN: 1-58112-435-X *(paperback)*
ISBN: 1-58112-436-8   *(eBook)*
rev b

BrownWalker.com

For Mary and the Fab Four - Lynde, Jenny, Curtis, and Coury. Thanks for your patience, support, and understanding. I hope this book justifies your many sacrifices.

ACKNOWLEDGMENT

There are many people that have inspired me in this effort. First, I must acknowledge the encouragement of Dr. Thomas Castellano at the Rochester Institute of Technology. His expertise and advice proved especially helpful. I also note the assistance of Drs. Kathy Ward, Jennifer Dunn, Jody Sundt and Michelle Miller at Southern Illinois University - Carbondale. Each lent their talents to this project. Special thanks must also be given to Dr. Rob Benford for his insight into the challenges and rewards of book writing.

Thanks are also given to the American Correctional Association, the U.S. Department of Justice, and the Criminal Justice Institute for their time and information.

CONTENTS

CHAPTER 3

**Inmate Litigation, the Judiciary, and
Perceptions of the Prison**   39

CHAPTER 5

PREFACE

This book has been a work in progress for the past decade. My interest in prisons and especially prison privatization was sparked while I was a student at the University of Nebraska. While there, I composed several papers on this subject. Little did I know that the prison in its many forms would become my future area of specialization. My interest in this topic has brought me into contact with many of today's most prominent penologists and practitioners. Many of these individuals have expressed concern about the direction being taken by the contemporary prison, especially the role that profit and privatization increasingly play.

My first professional experience with privatization occurred while employed at the Penitentiary of New Mexico at Santa Fe. While at PNM, I found myself part of a surreal world that few people encounter. I witnessed firsthand the need for improvement in the areas of inmate education, training, counseling, and treatment. This need for improvement was also recognized by correctional officials nationwide. State officials responded by privatizing many of New Mexico's prisons. Yet, as this process progressed, improvement seemed illusive. Concern remained about inmate treatment and the commercialization of punishment. I began to question the role of the prison within contemporary society and whether the benefits often attributed to privatization were real or merely hype.

As you read this book, recognize that it is based upon the belief that many inmates are changeable and that the prison by its very design was intended to be reform oriented. Only through effective inmate rehabilitation will society experience a reduction in prison expenditures. Any threat to this objective must be seen as a threat to society. Finally, consider the possibility that the prison's contemporary pursuit of profit may forever alter a system that while riddled with imperfections, has nonetheless traditionally operated with a degree of social awareness and accountability. Does it matter that prisons increasingly operate in a manner intended to maximize profit? Does profit as an operational objective fundamentally change the contemporary prison? Does public accountability help ensure ethical treatment? These are the types of questions that deserve consideration.

CHAPTER 1

Commodification in the
Contemporary Correctional Context

With the increased popularity of "get-tough" sanctions, demand for jail and prison space is great. As state and federal facilities are forced to exceed their designed capacity levels, solutions are increasingly being sought from the private sector. One popular solution is the privately operated facility. Under such an arrangement, a government jurisdiction pays a private company to confine inmates on its behalf. Data relating to the number of private facilities and their operating capacities vary widely by source. However, most suggest that there are in excess of 65,000 inmates being held in 140 private prison facilities. Other estimates place approximately 5 percent - 7 percent of the total U.S. inmate population within private facilities. To gain an appreciation for the extent of prison privatization, recognize that between 1995 and 2000, the capacity levels of state and federally operated prisons increased by 22 percent and 29 percent, respectively; however, the private sector experienced a capacity increase of 450 percent (Stephan & Karberg, 2003). Private facilities currently operate in Puerto Rico, the District of Columbia, and in 30 states. Texas has the most facilities (43), followed by California (24), Florida (10), and Colorado (9). The U.S. Bureau of Prisons has announced its intention to increase the number of federal prisoners housed in private prisons to an anticipated 20,000 within the next few years (Camp et al., 2002). In fact, in 2000, the Bureau of Prisons privatized 3,300 beds having an estimated value of $760 million over a 10-year period (Caplan, 2003).

The material that follows is largely limited to a consideration of the prison. This was done for several reasons. First, data are more readily available on this form of

1

confinement. Secondly, since prisons are guided by specific operational objectives, it is possible to determine if the public and private prison sectors adhere to similar or different ideologies. A consideration of the ideologies driving contemporary operations help illuminate changes that may be occurring within the prison. The current uncertainty about operational ideologies is resulting in a growing sense of doubt and dissatisfaction about modern penal practice. Not only is there confusion about the nature and purpose of the prison among the general citizenry, but confusion also exists among those employed by the prison itself. Historically, prison employees have justified various practices by placing them within established ideological frameworks. However, those now working in the prison often do so without the guidance of traditional ideologies. Instead, profit as an operational objective is gaining widespread endorsement.

Two Competing Ideologies

The ideologies of "normalization" and "less eligibility" are useful when considering prison operations. These ideologies permit a determination to be made about changes in the prison's ideological direction. Prisons that operate under the philosophy of normalization provide inmates with many freedoms and encourage responsible decision-making. Inmates are afforded a wide array of privileges and treatment options designed to minimize the harshness of the prison environment and prepare them for release. This philosophy values civil rights protections through both internal grievance procedures and judicial processes. Thus, normalization emphasizes an open style of management. Operators of these prisons provide employees with adequate amounts of training and pay to help ensure a dedicated, stable, and qualified staff.

In an opposite fashion, under the philosophy of "less eligibility" inmate rights are largely ignored, with few amenities being provided. Few opportunities are afforded for vocational, educational, or recreational participation. This approach emphasizes the punitive nature of the prison and stresses efficiency and informality in conflict resolution. Since informal modes of conflict resolution are valued, intervention by outsiders into disputes and matters related to prison operations is avoided. Instead, issues are addressed internally. Thus, a hallmark of these institutions is a closed approach to prison operations. Furthermore, inmates and staff are not seen as having an inherent worth, but are instead perceived as little more than participants in a much larger process. Therefore, individual characteristics or needs are of little concern to the prison's administration. In an attempt to ensure efficiency, staff are given minimum pay and training. Since this approach stresses efficiency, prefers to operate in a closed manner, and de-emphasizes inmate improvement initiatives, the likelihood for civil rights violations may be greater here than in prisons operating under the philosophy of normalization.

The characteristics of prison systems adhering to each of these philosophies are patterned in the following way:

Table 1.1   Operational Characteristics

Normalization	Less Eligibility
Decreased emphasis on efficiency	Increased emphasis on efficiency
Increased staff wages	Decreased staff wages
Increased staff to inmate ratios	Decreased staff to inmate ratios
Increased levels of staff training	Decreased levels of staff training
Increased staff retention rates	Decreased staff retention rates
Decreased levels of violence	Increased levels of violence
Suits less likely to be upheld	Suits more likely to be upheld

These ideologies provide a natural continuum upon which today's prisons can be situated. By placing normalization and less eligibility at opposite ends of this continuum, analysis

3

can reveal toward which ideology prisons generally fall. Such a determination helps reveal the ideological direction of the contemporary prison and helps identify similarities and differences existing between the public and private prison sectors. Thus, as operational characteristics are presented hereafter, a determination will be made about what each characteristic reveals about the prison's placement upon this continuum.

Socio-Economics and Incarceration

Before proceeding, it is important to realize that a great deal of uncertainty surrounds the operation of the contemporary prison. This observation becomes especially evident when considering the numerous contradictory ideologies that have surfaced in prison-related literature. Rehabilitation and offender reform, unlike other penological subjects, tends to receive little consideration. Even deterrence as an operational objective is now largely ignored. Instead, incapacitation and offender warehousing dominate penological discussion. Thus, many of the prison's traditional ideologies remain largely unexplored within a contemporary context. An attempt to gain an increased understanding of the prison helps fill a literary void in an age when incarceration is an increasingly popular sanction, and profit and efficiency are becoming dominate pursuits. Furthermore, when considering imprisonment, one must also recognize that it has a disproportionate impact upon the poor. In essence, a link exists between economics and incarceration. Therefore, to more fully understand imprisonment, it becomes necessary to consider it in conjunction with prevailing economic and political systems. For example, it has been observed that the government often protects the interest of the wealthy over the interests and rights of the poor and working classes. Those groups that dominate the economic and political spheres are better able to impose their will through the legal process. As

4

such, free-market systems can, and have sought profit in unusual and perhaps unethical ways. This observation fits particularly well into a consideration of incarceration as a profit-producing enterprise.

The realization that the poor and working class receive less government protection and are more often the target of enforcement efforts gained widespread acceptance in the 1960's when Americans began to view the government with skepticism. The belief that the government protects the values and interests of the powerful, while neglecting those of the average citizen, became popular. A great deal has been written about how the criminal justice system benefits the wealthy through the oppression of the poor. This is accomplished by a justice system that portrays crime as a product of the lower class. For one group to succeed another must fail; thus, the political system ensures that the affluent retain an advantageous position in relation to those possessing fewer resources and less ability to use the system for self-promotion. One way to retain an advantageous position is to place one's competitors at a disadvantage through imprisonment. Welch believes that the poor are currently being herded toward maintenance with the prison system (2000: 75), where 8 out of every 10 inmates are members of the lowest income level. When one considers that the contemporary prison largely fails to train or educate society's offenders, it becomes apparent that the prison helps perpetuate the cycle of poverty and disadvantage experienced by this group.

The belief that the "system" tends to benefit the affluent is further supported when one realizes that there have been relatively few efforts undertaken to directly protect the poor from government abuse. However, some of the most celebrated efforts include the judicial rulings made in *Mapp vs. Ohio* (1961; search), *Gideon vs. Wainwright* (1963; seizure), *Escobedo vs. Illinois* (1964; confessions) and *Miranda vs. Arizona* (1966; informed of rights). Other protections include those enacted by the legislature. For example, one of the most influential laws ever passed is the Civil Rights Act of 1871 (Ku

5

Klux Klan Act). This Act sought to protect newly freed slaves from reprisal. Emancipated African Americans represent one of the most disadvantaged groups ever known to North America. This Act attempted to ensure that the southern government extended the rights of full citizenship to the newly freed slave. In its contemporary version, this statute is known as Title 42: Section 1983 of the U.S. Federal Code. Title 42 permits all inmates, regardless of race, to file suit for a wide range of alleged mistreatment including those pertaining to medical needs, living conditions, due process violations, and religious freedoms. The ability of an inmate to hold prison operators legally and publicly accountable is often their only protection from abuse. This Act will be considered in much greater detail later, but for now a review of recent attempts to eliminate and severely weaken this Act is appropriate.

The Judicial Abandonment of the Prison

In the past, inmates were given a great deal of access to the judiciary. It was believed that this access would ensure the government's adherence to constitutional protections and prevailing standards of ethical treatment. Even though scholars assert that the prison has tended to operate with an interest in prisoner reform, public accountability was seen as the most appropriate way to ensure humane and constitutional conduct. This access is now being limited, due in part to the perception that inmate lawsuits are filed primarily for entertainment purposes. Lawsuits filed by inmates, even when lacking merit, prove costly with regard to defense preparation. Since suits are costly to address, questions persist as to whether inmates should be permitted continued access to the courts. Consider that in 1966 only 218 federally filed inmate lawsuits existed; however, by 1992 that number had climbed to almost twenty-seven thousand. This increase was instrumental in passage of the Civil Rights of Institutionalized Person's Act (CRIPA). This Act grants the Department of Justice the power to

6

investigate allegations of inmate mistreatment while emphasizing internal grievance procedures. Now internal mechanisms of dispute resolution rather than external forms that rely on legal accountability are increasingly utilized. This Act limits the court's ability to direct prison operations and shifts that responsibility to the executive branch. This shift is significant since it establishes a closed prison system that carries the government's full endorsement. A closed system that limits rights and freedoms increases the likelihood for inhumane and unconstitutional actions.

Similarly, the Prison Litigation Reform Act (PLRA) also seeks to reduce litigation and the court's involvement in prison operations. PLRA was signed into law on April 26, 1996 by President Bill Clinton as part of the Balanced Budget Downpayment Act II (HR 3019, Omnibus Appropriations Bill). Under this Act inmate complaints are addressed by officials of the same prison system to which the allegations pertain, effectively bypassing judicial review. Furthermore, PLRA prohibits the traditional waiving of fees for inmates filing complaints with the judiciary. This discourages lawsuits and makes it difficult or impossible for a large portion of the inmate population to obtain court assistance. This approach has been called "a departure from the traditional view of justice" (Luedtke v. Gudmanson [Wisconsin], 1997). Furthermore, no previous Act has ever attempted to so broadly and so completely limit the ability of the judiciary to protect the constitutional rights of the poor and disadvantaged. This Act also requires inmates that have had previous lawsuits dismissed as frivolous, malicious, or failing to state a claim for relief to be barred from further filings. PLRA has been quite effective in reducing judicial involvement in prison operations. For example, consider that in 1996, 42,215 suits were filed by inmates; however, by 1997, the first full year under PLRA, this number dropped to 28,247 – a reduction of 33 percent (Collins & Grant, 1998).

Both CRIPA and PLRA are significant since they reveal a move by the legislative branch to limit the inmate population's ability to seek judicial intervention. These Acts increase the likelihood for mistreatment and prison mismanagement since a closed system is neither accountable nor controllable. These Acts may also permit widespread regional variations to exist in prison operations. Without judicial intervention, operational uniformity will decrease giving rise to inconsistencies in ideals and standards pertaining to inmate treatment. Furthermore, inmate discipline could increasingly be based upon arbitrary criteria since prisons are now much freer to operate by the rules they themselves deem appropriate. Senators Kennedy and Simon expressed concern about PLRA during Senatorial debate on March 19, 1996:

> Mr. President, I rise to express my deep concern about the Title VIII of the pending appropriations bill, the so-called Prison Litigation Reform Act (PLRA). Its proponents say that the PLRA is merely an attempt to reduce frivolous prisoner litigation over trivial matters. In reality, the PLRA is a far-reaching effort to strip Federal Courts of the authority to remedy unconstitutional prison conditions. The PLRA is itself patently unconstitutional, and a dangerous legislative incursion into the world of the judicial branch. Finally, I note with great concern that the bill would set a dangerous precedent for stripping the federal courts of the ability to safeguard the civil rights of powerless and disadvantaged groups (Senator Kennedy).

> Mr. President, I join Senator Kennedy in raising my strong concerns about the Prison Litigation Reform Act, a section of S. 1594. In attempting to curtail frivolous prisoner

8

lawsuits, this litigation goes much too far, and instead may make it impossible for the Federal Courts to remedy constitutional and statutory violations in prisons, jails, and juvenile detention facilities ... No doubt there are prisoners who bring baseless suits that deserve to be thrown out of court. But unfortunately, in many instances there are legitimate claims that deserve to be addressed. History is replete with examples of egregious violations of prisoners' rights. These cases reveal abusive and inhumane treatment which cannot be justified no matter what the crime. In seeking to curtail frivolous lawsuits, we cannot deprive individuals of their basic civil rights. We must find the proper balance (Senator Simon).

CRIPA and PLRA take on even greater significance when one realizes that most organizations, especially those that pursue profit, prefer internal rather than external forms of conflict resolution. Internal processes effectively shield an organization from potentially damaging publicity as well as court ordered judgments. By limiting the ability of prisoners to seek judicial protection, civil rights violations will increase while the public's knowledge about these violations decrease. Thus, the judiciary is increasingly being forced to retreat from one of its most important tasks, the protection of society's weak. By decreasing the judiciary's ability to intervene in prison affairs, an environment is produced that is ideally suited for inmate commodification.

Commodification and Rehabilitation

Any serious consideration of the prison requires a review of the topics of inmate commodification and rehabilitation. For our use, commodification and rehabilitation are functional opposites. Commodification refers to approaching inmates as objects to be exploited in the pursuit of profit. As such, the rights and well being of the inmate are of little concern. Rehabilitation, on the other hand, seeks to initiate positive change within the inmate to produce a law-abiding citizen. As a process, rehabilitation is concerned with the long-term success of the inmate. Inmate success benefits society in reduced crime rates, reduced correctional expenditures and an overall healthier society. To understand the relationship between the prison and rehabilitation, it is necessary to consider the role that rehabilitation has traditionally played in the European and American prison. As early as the 16th century, prisons were attempting to address criminality through offender reform. These institutions sought to produce a productive citizenry by providing inmates with work-related skills. It was believed that skill development would help the offender escape a criminal lifestyle. Later, prisons attempted to rehabilitate offenders through separation, corrective discipline, labor and an intense religious regime. Evidence suggests that a rehabilitative ideology had taken hold in Europe prior to the 17th century and an "argument can be made that enthusiasm for rehabilitation as a major objective of penal sanctions dates back to the time of Plato or before" (Thomas, 1987). Thus, historically there exists a relationship between the prison and offender reform.

Colonial America also embraced rehabilitation. Early Americans expected criminal sanctions to stress rehabilitation and offender reform. In general, colonial sanctions were more lenient than were those of other nations. For example, the Massachusetts and Pennsylvania colonies sought imprisonment for their offenders rather than the more harsh forms of corporal and capital punishments prescribed under traditional

10

English law. This approach suggests that colonists valued the reformative power of the prison; if they hadn't, they would have chosen corrective actions that could have been administered much more quickly and cheaply. William Paley's, *"Principles of Moral and Political Philosophy"* (1785) not only helped establish the early prison system but also stressed the importance of rehabilitation. Later in 1787, a group of colonial leaders met at the home of Benjamin Franklin and officially recognized rehabilitation as a penal objective. At the National Prison Association's meeting in 1870 (now called the American Correctional Association), the nation's leading penologists affirmed rehabilitation as the prison's primary objective.

Presently, rehabilitation has lost a great deal of support. The decline in rehabilitation's popularity is traceable to the 1970's when scholars pronounced offender reform unobtainable. Admittedly, from a financial perspective, rehabilitative programs prove costly. Of all the objectives of the prison, rehabilitation is by far the most expensive to achieve and the most difficult to quantify. This expense and the related difficulty of implementing these programs have led to a contemporary de-emphasis on rehabilitation. This de-emphasis has had a substantial impact upon the prison. In essence, it has freed the prison from its external expectations and has instead encouraged it to become more internally oriented. The prison has begun to measure its success not in terms of recidivism, but by any means it desires; whether that is by the number of inmates it incarcerates, the number of days without staff injury, even profit. Internal measures are becoming the criterion of choice for gauging prison performance.

The degree to which rehabilitation has lost support becomes evident when considering current sentencing requirements. These requirements now mandate imprisonment for a greater number of crimes, making imprisonment the current sanction of choice. Therefore, the traditional caveat that it is best to reserve imprisonment for the dangerous and habitual offender and sentence all others to community-based sanctions is being abandoned. In 1980, approximately 46 percent of those individuals convicted in U.S. District Courts received prison sentences; by 2001, 74 percent received a term of imprisonment (Bureau of Justice Statistics, 2001), an increase of approximately 30 percent. Similar rates of incarceration are also seen at the local and state levels. This indicates a nationwide move toward greater use of the second most severe sanction available - imprisonment. Not only is the prison being used more frequently, but sentence length has increased. Increases in sentence length can be seen nationwide where recent changes have doubled and even tripled sentence length for many felony convictions. The increased use of imprisonment and increases in sentence length have resulted in large prison populations. In 1980, there were 319,598 inmates in the nation's prison system. By 2002, that number had grown to approximately 1,367,856 (Bureau of Justice Statistics, 2003). Thus, over the past twenty-five years, the U.S. prison population has increased four-fold. Congress has even tied federal funds for state prison construction to the requirement of increased sentence length (Pub.L.No. 103-322, 108 Stat. 1796 (1994).

Furthermore, by introducing profit into the prison, a change occurs in the identity of the prison's beneficiaries (Shichor, 1999). For example, traditional prison operations made society and the inmate both beneficiaries of its programs. Offender reform assisted the inmate by providing the skills necessary for maintaining a law-abiding lifestyle, while attempting to make society safer by lowering recidivism rates. However, under a system that emphasizes profit, the prison's beneficiaries become those that financially benefit from its success including its owners, shareholders, and employees. Under a profit ideology, the success of the prison itself becomes paramount, and not the future success of its inmates. As profit is incorporated into the organizational structure of the prison, it emerges as the dominant goal and becomes the sole measure of success. A cost-to-benefit-analysis is conducted prior to every action, ensuring that the prison will only behave in a manner that proves financially rewarding. One way that prison operators have begun to seek greater profit is though the use of inmate labor. While inmate labor has historically been linked to rehabilitation, it is now increasingly undertaken with little regard for its therapeutic or educational benefit.

Inmate Labor

The relationship between the modern prison and inmate labor is well documented. In fact, the factory (a bastion of hard labor) and the penitentiary emerged simultaneously. Initially, inmate labor was viewed as a way to train offenders to be future factory workers, thus giving inmates employable skills. In many ways, prison labor programs closely imitated the factory. If prisons did not operate in-house work programs, they often leased-out their inmates to local industry or business establishments. Oftentimes leased-out inmates were not compensated for their labor; however, if an inmate managed to exceed the required minimum output, "as a rule, received a small sum of money with which they could buy extras" (Spierenburg, 1998: 64). Of course, this incentive helped motivate inmates toward increased productivity. As the prison evolved, the use of inmate labor as well as its resulting benefits were reserved for the government itself. To illustrate this fact, consider that in 1885, 75 percent of all prison inmates were involved in work programs with most of them working for various private companies. However, by 1935 only 10 percent worked for the private sector (National Center for Policy Analysis, 2001) with the remainder being employed by the public prison system. Thus, the government began to realize the potential value associated with inmate labor.

The government's monopoly on the use of inmates as a labor source has recently been relaxed. For example, between 1980 and 1994, the number of inmates employed by private companies jumped 358 percent with overall profits exceeding

$1.3 billion (Kicenski, 1998; Erlich, 1995). Thirty states now permit inmates to work for corporations that include, or have included, Microsoft, Victoria's Secret, IBM, and TWA (Cohen, 1996; Christie, 2000).

Furthermore, the free market sale of inmate produced goods, which was traditionally prohibited, has now been repealed. The Hawes Cooper (1934) and Ashurst Sumner (1935) Acts that historically protected inmates from free-market exploitation and unfair labor practices are no longer in effect. These Acts prohibited the commercial sale of inmate-produced goods between states and made their transportation across state lines a federal offense. The repeal of these Acts has intimately and perhaps permanently linked inmate labor to profit. In 1979 the Percy Amendment (Justice System Improvement Act) was passed permitting the sale of inmate-produced products between states. Now states can sell goods to each other for profit. Similarly, in 1990, Proposition 139 was approved in California permitting private firms to utilize inmate labor to produce and sell goods on the open market. Since passage, California has exported prisoner made clothing internationally. The mission statement by California's own Prison Industry Authority (PIA) specifies that their programs will strive to produce and sell goods for profit (PIA, 1992). Other ventures include Oregon's "Prison Blues" line of clothing. Oregon's prisoners make jeans that are marketed with slogans such as, "Made on the inside to be worn on the outside." One advertisement shows "Prison Blues" jeans and the electric chair with the caption – "Sometimes our jeans last longer than the guys who make them." These activities clearly show that profit is now a pursuit of the prison. This has led to concerns about the commercial aspects of imprisonment. At the center of these concerns lies the possibility that inmates will be viewed as commodities with their labor being bought and sold for commercial purposes. Milton Friedman, a Chicago School economist recognizes that, "the corporation [whether publicly or privately operated] can not be ethical. Its only responsibility is to turn a profit" (Peck, 2001: 1). Thus, ethics, ideals of fair treatment, and adherence to civil rights protections may become secondary to profit itself. This possibility is addressed in the following statement:

> profits are more than viable when inmates, who often earn between $.23 and $1.15 an hour, have as their only competition foreign-based labor (who in some ways are becoming more costly to utilize) who have been exploited by corporate entities for decades on the basis of some of the same advantages offered by prison inmates: a non-unionized work force, no minimum wage, no benefits, no healthcare, no worker's compensation, and finally, no commitment to employment longer than is advantageous to a clear profit margin (Kicenski, 1998: 4).

With the American rate of incarceration being perhaps the highest in the world (approximately 600 in 100,000), where but in our prisons could workers be found with many of the same beneficial characteristics long associated with third-world laborers? Inmate laborers are being "transformed into the functional equivalent of foreign workers" (Weiss, 2001: 270). Both represent groups that are powerless, captive, and largely poor and illiterate. In fact, one Oregon State Representative suggested that corporations form alliances with prison systems just as they do with overseas labor markets. Similarly, the Federal Inmate Work Act of 2001 authorizes private companies to utilize, "federal inmate labor to produce items that would otherwise be produced by foreign labor" (Federal Inmate Work Act, 2001). This approach exposes a willingness by lawmakers, prison officials and private industry to use inmate populations as a source of cheap and captive labor.

Summary

Prison privatization is not a recent innovation. In fact, privatization is a practice that extends to the very roots of early European and American prisons. Over time, governments monopolized prison operation and assumed sole responsibility for the law-breaker. It wasn't until the mid-1980's that prison privatization re-emerged in response to exploding prison populations and dwindling public budgets. Privatization raises concerns about how profit may impact the traditional objectives of the prison. Of particular concern is how profit may effect inmate treatment. Concerns of this nature take on special significance when one views them in connection with recent legislation that limits and even eliminates the judiciary's ability to enforce constitutional and humanitarian mandates within the prison. Finally, with the ability of prison operators to produce and sell goods without restriction, questions about commercialized incarceration and captive labor persists.

Discussion Questions

1). Which operational ideology is better suited to rehabilitation and inmate reform? Why?

2). Should the prison attempt to break the cycle of poverty and unemployment experienced by an overwhelming number of its inmates?

3). What is the significance of CRIPA and PLRA?

4). What is the difference between commodification and rehabilitation?

5). How might a profit rationale change the prison? Is it reasonable to believe that the success of the inmate will become secondary to the success of the prison itself?

6). What are two concerns associated with the commercialized use of inmate labor?

Sources

Bureau of Justice Statistics, 2003. *Number of persons in custody of state correctional prisons.*

------ 2001. *Trends in the outcomes of cases concluded in U.S. district court.*

Camp, S., G. Gaes & William Saylor, 2002. "Quality of prison operations in the US federal sector." *Punishment & Society*, 4 (1).

Cohen, Warren, 1996. "Need work? Go to jail". *U.S. News Online.* http://www.usnews.com/issue/9prison

Collins, William & Darlene Grant, 1998. "The Prison Litigation Reform Act." *Corrections Today* (8) pp. 60-62.

Caplan, J. 2003. "Policy for profit: The private-prison industry's influence over criminal justice legislation." *ACJS Today* 26: 15.

Christie, Nels, 2000. *Crime control as industry.* Routledge Press 3rd ed.

Erlich, Reese, 1995. 'Prison labor: Working for the man". *Covert Action Quarterly* (54).

Federal Inmate Work Act, 2001. 107th Congress 1st Session S. 1228

Kicenski, Karyl, 1998. *The corporate prison: The production of crime and the sale of discipline.* George Mason University.

National Center for Policy Analysis, 2001. *Crime and punishment in America.* Study 193

National Institute of Justice, 1987. *Issues in contracting for the private operation of prisons and jails.* Washington, D.C.; US Department of Justice

Peck, John, 2001. *Keeping your school clean of suits and spooks: How to research, challenge, and eliminate military and corporate influence on campus.*
http//:www.corporations.org/democracy/spoooks.html
.

Prison Industry Authority, *Mission statement,* 1992. Annual Report Fiscal Years 1991-1992.

Shichor, David, 1999. "Privatizing correctional institutions: An organizational perspective". *The Prison Journal,* 79 (2).

Stephan, J., & J. C. Karberg. 2003. *Census of state and federal correctional facilities, 2003.* Washington, DC: U.S. Department of Justice.

Thomas, Charles, 1987. *Corrections in America - Problems of the past and the present.* Sage Publications.

Weiss, Robert, 2001. "Repatriating low-wage work: The political economy of prison labor reprivatization in the post Industrial United States". *Criminology,* 39 (2).

Welch, Michael, 2000. "The role of the immigration and naturalization service in the prison-industrial complex". *Social Justice:* 27 (3).

CHAPTER 2

The Private Sector

The reliance upon government to address crime is a relatively recent development. In fact, for most of human history the protection of life and property was a private matter. English law, from which American law derived, is based upon Anglo-Saxon custom. Under Anglo-Saxon custom, individuals living in small kindred and tribal units relied upon the group for the apprehension and punishment of offenders. Furthermore, before the 10th century the use of private detention was common. Operators of these private facilities sought profit and self-sufficiency by charging fees for their services. Fees were routinely charged for food, laundry, and even release. In fact, Jeremy Bentham's panopticon (1780's) was intended to be privately operated with Bentham campaigning "tirelessly to obtain this contract for himself" (Christie, 2000: 120). As government became more complex, publicly operated prisons became the norm, forcing the private sector to the periphery of prison operations. There, it became adept at providing the public prison with a variety of specialty and support services. Some of these include education and training, kitchen and food preparation, and laundry services. Thus, the private prison entered a state of dormancy awaiting its opportunity to re-emerge.

The groundwork for privatization's re-emergence dates to the 1960's when there arose a social desire to reduce the size of the government and limit its control over the citizenry. This movement was fueled by a growing dissatisfaction with government and its inability to fulfill its responsibilities. The trend to privatize prisons began in earnest in 1984 when jurisdictions in Tennessee and Florida began to privately house inmates. Later, a private corporation attempted to secure a statewide contract in Tennessee. After negotiations faltered, Kentucky (1985) became the first State to enter into an agreement with a private prison operator. Within six years, there were 15,000 private prison beds in existence in the United States. By 1996, this number had increased by over 400 percent. Furthermore, during 1996, Corrections Corporation of America (a private correctional company often described as the industry leader) either operated or was constructing facilities to house 40,000 inmates, making it the sixth largest prison system within the United States. The shift toward a hybrid system that uses both public and private prisons has led to concern about an inherent conflict between social and corporate interests. One area that has received little consideration is the effect of privatization upon the prison employee. Therefore, a consideration of the differences that exist between the sectors with regard to staff proves enlightening.

Prison Staff
Salary, Training Levels, and Staffing Ratio's

A full consideration of the effect of privatization upon prison staff requires an examination of salary levels. Little data exists that permit comparisons to be made between the sectors, but what is available reveals some striking differences. For example, in 1998, the private sector paid officers an average starting salary of $15,919 to a maximum salary of $19,103 per year. This range represents a difference of $3,184. In comparison, the public sector paid new officers an average of $21,246 to a maximum of $34,004 per year (Criminal Justice Research Institute, 1998). This range represents a difference of $12,758 and reveals that the private sector tends to pay new officers approximately $5,000 less per year than the public sector, with a difference in maximum salaries being about $15,000.

Similarly, in 2000, the salary of an entry-level private officer was an average $19,344 per year, compared to $21,855 per year for the public officer – a difference of $2,511 per year.

When comparing the maximum salary of both the private and public officer, we see these figures increase to $21,790 and $34,728, respectively - an annual difference of about $13,000 or about $1100 per month (AFSCME, 2000; Austin & Coventry, 2001: 47; Criminal Justice Institute, 2000). These figures reveal that the private sector offers both a lower starting salary and less potential for salary advancement than does the public sector. Lower pay and a reduced ability to increase one's salary may have a direct effect upon the caliber of employee that the private sector is able to attract and retain (see Table 2.2). Based solely upon a consideration of staff wages, it appears that the private sector adheres more closely to the ideology of less eligibility than does the public sector.

Furthermore, profit dictates that the private sector employ as few staff as possible. With labor accounting for approximately 70 percent of a prison's operating costs, greater inmate-to-staff ratios would, in turn, produce greater profit. For inmate-to-staff ratios, the private sector reports an average 6.7 inmates per officer and 3.7 inmates per staff member. The public sector in comparison reports an average 5.6 inmates per correctional officer and 3.1 inmates per staff member (Criminal Justice Institute, 1998). Thus, the private sector does indeed operate with a higher inmate-to-staff ratio. Generally, it is recognized that private prisons operate with 15 to 50 percent fewer staff than do publicly operated prisons. For example, lawmakers in North Carolina learned that Corrections Corporation of America (CCA) planned to employ only 68 officers to supervise 528 inmates instead of the 141 officers the State would have itself employed (Neff, 1998). Using the public officer's starting salary of $21,246 as a test of savings, this example reveals that CCA would have profited $1.5 million in annual operating expenses simply by having a higher inmate to officer ratio. Even private juvenile facilities operate, on average, with twice the number of inmates per staff member than does the public sector (3.9 vs. 1.7) (Armstrong & MacKenzie, 2003). Based upon staffing patterns, it appears that the private sector is nearer the less eligibility end of the

22

ideological continuum than is the public sector.

The following Table provides information related to each sector's facilities, inmates, and staff. Note that from 1995 to 2000, the largest increase in type of confinement was in the private sector (Stephan & Karberg, 2003). Furthermore, regardless of whether the unit of analysis is prisons, inmates, or staff, increases were dramatically higher for the private sector than for either the state or federal systems. This information proves useful when considering salary, staffing, and training patterns.

Table 2.1   Number of Facilities*, Inmates, Rated Capacity, and Staff in Federal, State, and Private Prisons, 1995 and 2000

Number of facilities	1995	2000
Federal	75	84
State	1,056	1,023
Private	29	101
Rated capacity		
Federal	64,500	83,113
State	891,826	1,090,225
Private	18,294	105,133
Number of inmates		
Federal	80,221	110,974
State	899,376	1,055,746
Private	12,736	77,854

Table 2.1   Continued

Number of staff

Federal	10,048	12,376
State	207,647	243,352
Private	3,197	14,589

---

* These facilities permit less than 50% of their residents to regularly leave unaccompanied by staff.

Source: Stephan, J. J., and J. C. Karberg. 2003. *Census of state and federal correctional facilities, 2002.* Washington, DC: U.S. Department of Justice.

Table 2.2 Reasons for Staff Turnover in Private and Public Prisons

	Private Prisons	Public Prisons
Resigned	71%	63%
Retired	0.6%	15%
Fired/Other	28.4%	22%

Source: *Criminal Justice Institute, 1998.*

But what about employee training? Well, let's consider pre-service training which is given to newly hired employees prior to their initial assignment. In 1998, the private sector provided its new officers with an average of 174 hours. In comparison, the public sector provided its new officers with an average of 232 hours. Thus, the public sector provided 58 additional hours of pre-service training beyond that which the private sector provided its employees (Criminal Justice Institute, 1998). Similarly, in 2000, public officers received an average of 240 hours of pre-service training compared to 177 for private officers, a difference of 63 hours (AFSCME, 2000; Greene, 2000; Logan, 1990). With regard to annual in-service training, little or no difference between the sectors appears to exist. Based solely upon a consideration of pre-service training, the private sector appears to be nearer the less eligibility end of the ideological continuum than is the public sector.

What effect, if any, do these differences have? Well, an argument might be made that lower salaries, less advancement opportunities, fewer staff, and reduced training levels might collectively act to produce a more dangerous prison. Therefore, lets consider "assault frequency" as a measure of each sector's level of dangerousness.

Prison Dangerousness

For our purposes, an assault is considered to have occurred when an inmate causes another person bodily injury. In 1998, the private sector experienced an average of 40 assaults on inmates and 9 assaults on staff per prison. During this same time period, the public sector experienced 19 assaults on inmates and 10 assaults on staff per prison. Thus, the private sector experienced in excess of twice the number of assaults on inmates and slightly fewer assaults on staff than did the public sector. These figures suggest that the private sector is a more dangerous place to be incarcerated, and a slightly safer place to be employed. Furthermore, these findings are particularly noteworthy when considering each sector's operating capacity and the dangerousness of their inmate populations.

Three characteristics often correlated with a prison's assault rate are the average age of the inmate population, facility crowding, and inmate dangerousness. As you may expect, young inmates are more likely to resort to violence or be the targets of a violent act than are inmates that are older and correspondingly better established. Frequently, young inmates have simply not developed appropriate coping mechanisms for dealing with the stresses of incarceration. Furthermore, prisons with inmate populations that exceed designed capacity levels heighten competition for such scarce resources as job and educational opportunities, staff attention, and even personal space. Increased competition breeds increases in aggression and the potential for violence. With increased inmate-to-staff ratios, the opportunity for employees to effectively detect and intervene in potentially violent situations decrease. Similarly, each sector's proclivity toward violence can be roughly estimated by simply considering the security designation of its prisons. For example, one would assume that a higher security prison is generally more dangerous than a lower security prison. In essence, classification procedures are expected to identify inmates with histories of violence or the potential for violence and assign them to an appropriate facility. Thus, it would be expected that inmates and staff in high security prisons would experience violence at greater frequencies than do inmates and staff at low security prisons. Therefore, the sector that operates the greatest proportion of high security prisons also likely experiences higher assault rates (supermax or total lockdown-facilities excluded). Since no distinguishable differences exist in the average age of either sector's inmate population, we shall briefly consider facility crowding and inmate dangerousness.

Table 2.3   Demographic, Custody, and Sentencing Data

Characteristic	Private %	Public %
Race		
African American	42.8	47.4
White	31.9	43.3
Other/Unknown	25.3	9.3
Gender		
Male	90.0	93.6
Female	10.0	6.4
Age at Admission	30 yrs.	31 yrs.
% 49 or less	94	92.8
% 50 or older	6	7.2
Custody Levels*		
% Maximum	5.9	26.5
% Medium	42.7	36.7
% Minimum	47.3	32.4
Av. Months Served		
by releasees	11.3	27.7
% Capacity	82	113

Due to the exclusion of facilities housing less than 100 inmates, custody figures total 95%. Custody level reflects the percentage of the inmate population so designated.

During 1998, private prisons operated at 82 percent capacity. Simply stated, 82 out of every 100 private prison beds were occupied, leaving 18 out of every 100 empty. The public sector, however, operated at 113 percent capacity, revealing its prisons to be more crowded than are those of the private sector. Based solely upon this characteristic, one would expect the public sector to experience greater levels of violence. Similarly, an institution's dangerousness is reflected in its security level. Thus, the sector that operates the greatest proportion of higher security institutions should also experience a high rate of assault. Nine out of every 10 private prisons are either minimum or medium security facilities; whereas, 7 out of every 10 public prisons are similarly classified. More specifically, the private sector has only 6 percent of its inmate population housed in maximum security, while the public sector has over a quarter of its inmates similarly housed (see Table 2.3). This suggests that as a general practice, the public sector retains those offenders believed to be the most dangerous or potentially violent. Again, considering this characteristic, one would expect the private prison to be a safer place to be incarcerated. However, this is not the case. Therefore, based solely upon assault rates, the private sector, despite factors that suggest that it should experience less violence, is in reality more dangerous. This finding places the private sector nearer the less eligibility end of the ideological continuum than is the public sector.

The lack of publicized information about private sector violence may demonstrate a growing level of ambivalence toward our inmate populations. The safety of our inmates may be of less importance than efficient and profitable operations. To examine this possibility, a closer consideration of the financial and political factors surrounding privatization is in order.

Financial Factors

With the increased use of imprisonment as a criminal sanction, correctional budgets nationwide have been severely strained. This strain has helped make privatization's promise of financial savings appealing. Concern about the cost of imprisonment became evident as early as the 1970's when publicly operated correctional departments became concerned with justifying their existence. This was necessary because of the growing number of claims about the government's fiscal mismanagement. Claims of fiscal mismanagement have convinced many public officials that free enterprise and the privatization of traditional government services is the most appropriate mechanism to obtain cost-effective operations. In fact, the private sector has capitalized upon this perception by boldly touting its ability to efficiently operate prisons. These statements often claim that they can avoid typical restrictions that encumber the public sector and increase operating costs. In fact, private operators do evade many of the restrictions that prevent the government from more cheaply operating its prisons. For example, the private sector avoids civil service procedures pertaining to the hiring, firing, promotion, and the salary and benefit's packages provided public employees. When employee benefits can be avoided, significant decreases in operating costs result.

With all this talk about efficiency, how much can a jurisdiction realistically save through privatization? Many sources suggest that the savings attributed to private operations range from 5 to 20 percent. One of the most widely cited studies on operational savings was conducted in the 1980's and involved Corrections Corporation of America (CCA). CCA assumed management of a 350-bed minimum/medium security prison located in Chattanooga, Tennessee. The facility was deteriorated, neglected, and was in need of major renovation. Since Hamilton County spent less on its correctional costs than its regional counterparts and due to the poor condition of its facility, it was believed that any analysis comparing the costs of public and private operations would provide a rigorous test of cost savings. This study concluded that over a three-year period, costs were reduced by approximately 15 percent (Logan, 1990).

Stories within the news media also abound with regard to savings. One article appearing in the *Columbus Dispatch* (2000: 5c) details a private contractor that promised to save Ohio $1.1 million over a 21-month period. Furthermore, in an extensive and widely-publicized study (Pratt & Maahs, 1999), findings revealed that the cost to house an inmate within a privately operated facility was $2.45 less per day than it was to house an inmate in a public facility. This amounts to approximately $900.00 per inmate, per year. For a 500-bed prison, the savings would be $447,125 per year. Although this finding supports the contention that incarceration by the private sector is less expensive, the promise of immense savings or the alleviation of large financial burdens on state correctional budgets have not materialized to the extent previously purported. Furthermore, findings indicate that it is not the sector operating the prison that matters; rather operating expenses more directly correlate with a facility's age and security level. With the private sector operating newer and lower security facilities, savings would be expected. A nationwide study conducted by the U.S. Marshals Service found that their use of privately operated facilities were actually costing 24 percent more than were those facilities operated by the public sector (Gerth & Labaton, 1995). More recently, Austin and Coventry (2001) found that savings provided by privatization were almost nonexistent.

To further reduce costs, prison operators nationwide have begun to impose inmate pay provisions. This practice requires inmates to subsidize prison operators for a wide array of services. Such a practice indicates an attempt by both sectors to discourage the use of various prison services and to increase efficiency by sharing operating costs with inmate populations. Current figures reveal that approximately 68 percent of privately operated prisons charge inmates for health care services, with 32 percent providing health care services free of charge. Fees frequently range from an average low of $3.00 per visit to an average maximum of $3.75. Similarly, 65 percent of the publicly operated prisons charge fees for health care services with 35 percent providing these services free of charge. The fees charged by public prisons range from an average low of $2.85 per visit to an average maximum of $3.09. Thus, both sectors now charge inmates for services that were freely provided just a few short years ago. The preliminary popularity of these programs suggests that their use will increase.

Not only are prison operators now considering the financial aspects of incarceration to a greater extent than before, but so too is the public. Prisons are increasingly viewed as economic centerpieces in many communities. In fact, communities nationwide have responded to the prospect of acquiring new prisons by lauding corporate leaders and politicians with gifts and other forms of favoritism. For example, in the late 1990's, Florida officials promoted their state's anticipated building of additional prisons with color brochures claiming that a 1,100 bed prison was worth $25 million a year and 350 jobs to each community fortunate enough to be selected. "Towns responded by lining up for the chance at such a bounty" (Lotke, 1996: 1). Similarly, the private sector has also done its share of courting interested communities. One example includes the now infamous 1995 American Jail Association's conference promoting privatization with the slogan of, "Tap into the Sixty-Five Billion Dollar Jails Market." A similar convention in 1996 promoted itself with the slogan, "Private Correctional Facilities – Private Prisons, Maximize Investment Returns in This Exploding Industry" (Welch, 1999: 277; Shichor, 1999: 232). Both of these slogans indicate the manner by which society is beginning to view the prison as a means to economic profitability and community development. With claims of efficiency and economic stimulus, the private sector is in a position to more permanently entrench itself within corrections through involvement in the political process.

Politics and Prison Privatization

It is no secret that governments worldwide have experienced significant political influence by corporations. To maintain and even increase profitability, the private sector has also sought to influence various political processes. This influence ensures that the private prison sector's interests are considered during policy and legislative undertakings and that it maintains and even expands operations. In fact, the private sector may eventually influence our nation's prison systems to the same extent as the defense industry is influenced by Lockheed Martin and McDonnell Douglas (Lotke, 1996). Influence can occur through a lobbying mechanism designed to win the support of politicians, political groups, and academicians. This process, at times, disregards moral, ethical and public interest concerns. Since lobbying is a self-promoting activity, concern exists that the private sector will pursue its specific interests to the detriment of society. Consider this statement:

> The most worrisome aspect of prison privatization is the inevitable emergence of a private "prison lobby" concerned not with social welfare but with increasing its dividends, not with doing good, but doing well. Sentencing guidelines, parole rules, corrections budgets, and new criminal legislation are areas in which private prison operators have a vested interest and could influence policy decisions (Smith, 1993: 6).

The criminal justice system may, in fact, be at risk for manipulation. Welch envisions a "cohort" of politicians, business leaders and private contractors that lobby for a system that provides them with financial benefits (2000). Just such an example is obtained from Tennessee where politicians attempted to privatize the entire state prison system, a $200 million deal. Later it was discovered that the Governor's wife (Honey Alexander) and the Speaker of the House (Ned McWherter) were stockholders in the private company vying for the contract. Furthermore, the private lobbyist involved in this process was married at one time to the Speaker of the House. This case reveals how several of Tennessee's political "insiders" were nearly successful in manipulating the political process for personal gain. It also reveals how personal gain and the promise of "profit" can supplant public interests.

The private sector has, in fact, spared little expense to win the favor of politicians and government officials (Greene, 2000). To effectively influence these individuals, lobbyists are often drawn from a pool of former legislators that posses a distinct advantage in obtaining access to current public leaders. The private sector's ability to influence the political process lies in its capability to employ former officials. Shichor refers to employing former officials as the "revolving door syndrome" – whereby those in the private sector hire well-connected "insiders" (1999: 239 & 240). Additional influence is sought through campaign contributions. Even President Bush and former-presidential candidate Gore accepted substantial donations from private operators (Nader, 2000). It is through these activities that prison operations are increasingly becoming tied to private interests.

Private corporations are also exerting a great deal of influence through funding research. Since the 1970's the private business sector has increasingly become involved in forming working relationships with universities and academicians. This movement has been called the "corporatization of higher education" (Peck, 2001: 1). Since 1981, private funding to universities has increased approximately five-fold, topping $1.7 billion (Peck, 2001). One example of how the private prison sector has itself engaged in this type of activity involves Professor Charles Thomas. Thomas, a noted university researcher, was widely considered one of America's leading experts on prison privatization. Much of Thomas' research supported privatization and heralded its benefits. After promoting privatization for years, Thomas was publicly accused of being dishonest in his claim of being an independent advocate. Later, it was discovered that a private operator had funneled $400,000 into his research (Lilly, 1998). Thomas also had a substantial amount of money invested in private prisons and was receiving $12,000 a year to serve on the board of one corporation. Other reports claim that Thomas received a three million-dollar fee for his support (Greene, 2000). While the total dollar amount received for his various endorsements will never be known, Thomas eventually resigned his tenured professorship at the University of Florida and admitted violating ethics laws. This example clearly shows the desire of the private sector to shape public policy by funding research "paid" to promote its interests. While political lobbying and academic endorsements are becoming more common, the primary difference between efforts undertaken by the private prison sector and those of other industry is that one deals with the depravation of freedom and liberties, and the application of pain and discomfort, whereas the others do not. This is a fundamental difference that should not be overlooked.

Summary

Staff and inmates alike will remain targets for commodification and exploitation (by both sectors) for as long as society seeks efficient and profitable forms of incarceration. It is likely that prison privatization will remain a popular form of imprisonment. Currently, commercialized incarceration is resulting in reduced salary and training levels for private officers. Private prisons also operate with fewer staff per inmate than do public prisons. The full effects of privatization upon the correctional employee and inmate have yet to be determined. A good deal of information pertaining to these issues must still be inferred from limited data concerning operational characteristics. Increased insight into prison operations can be gleaned form a consideration of judicial processes. Of particular interest are those allegations cited within inmate litigation and their respective judicial findings.

Discussion Questions

1). What factors may have contributed to the re-emergence of prison privatization?

2). Of the differences that exist between the private and public prison sectors, which two do you find to be the most significant? Why?

3). What factors are associated with prison violence?

4). Compare and contrast the lobbying efforts of the private prison sector with similar efforts by other forms of industry. Could these efforts have negative effects for society?

Sources

AFSCME - American Federation of State, County and Municipal Employees, 2000. *Public and private prisons compared.* http://www.afscme.org/private/98rbk.htm.

Armstrong, G., & D. MacKenzie. 2003. Private vs. public juvenile correctional facilities: Do differences in environmental quality exist? *Crime and Delinquency* 49: 542-563.

Austin, James & Garry Coventry, 2001. *Emerging issues on privatized prisons.* U.S. Department of Justice/Bureau of Justice Assistance: NCJ 181249.

Christie, Nels, 2000. *Crime control as industry.* Routledge Press, 3rd ed.

Columbus (OH) Dispatch, 3/21/00. "Union says new private prisons guilty of misusing state workers."

Criminal Justice Institute, 2000. *The 1998 corrections yearbook: Adult corrections.* Middleton, CT.

Gerth, J., & S. Labaton, 1995. Prisons for profit. *New York Times*, November 24.

Greene, Judith, 2000. *Prison privatization: Recent developments in the United States.* Paper presented at the International Conference on Penal Abolition.

Lilly, Robert, 1998. "Private prisons in the US." *Prison Service Journal*, 120.

Logan, Charles, 1990. *Private prisons: Cons and pros.* Oxford University Press, New York. Pp. 41-48.

Lotke, Eric, 1996. "The prison-industrial complex." *Multinational Monitor*: November 17(11).

Nader, Ralph, 2000. *Nader tells corporations to get out of the prison industry.* A speech presented to Youngstown State University (Ohio) on September 27th.

Neff, J. 1998. *Lawmakers want to let a private-prison company double the capacity of the facilities it is building.* http://www.afscme/private/crimep03.htm.

Peck, John, 2001. *Keeping your school clean of suits and spooks: How to research, challenge, and eliminate military and corporate influence on campus.* www.corporations.org/democracy.

Pratt, Travis & Jeff Maahs, 1999. Are private prisons more cost-effective than public prisons? A meta-analysis of evaluation research studies. *Crime and Delinquency*.

Shichor, David, 1999. "Privatizing correctional institutions: An Organizational Perspective." *The Prison Journal*, 79 (2).

Smith, Phil, 1993. *"Private prisons: Profit of crime".* *Covert Action Quarterly* (Fall Issue).

Stephan, J., & J. C. Karberg. 2003. *Census of state and federal correctional facilities, 2003.* Washington, DC: U.S. Department of Justice.

Welch, Michael, 2000. "The role of the Immigration and Naturalization Service in the prison-industrial complex." *Social Justice*: 27 (3).

------ 1999. *Punishment in America: Social control and the ironies of imprisonment.* Thousand Oaks, CA: Sage.

CHAPTER 3

Inmate Litigation, the Judiciary, and
Perceptions of the Prison

Even though modern private prisons have been in operation since the mid-1980s, relatively little is known about how they approach inmates and staff. This lack of knowledge is significant since speculation about private operations abound within the literature. A substantial portion of this speculation suggests that incarceration by the private sector is of a lower quality than that provided by the public sector. This position is based upon the belief that profit has a negative effect upon the operational characteristics of the prison. Conversely, speculation also exists, albeit to a lesser extent, suggesting that privatization promotes humanitarian and constitutional treatment as a means to avoid bad publicity and civil judgments. These divergent perspectives indicate uncertainty about private sector operations in general, and more specifically, about the legal challenges that confront the contemporary prison.

When considering the legal challenges confronting the contemporary prison, it is necessary to recognize the role played by the Civil Rights Act of 1871 (Ku Klux Klan Act). This Act represents the most significant attempt ever undertaken to protect the civil rights of the poor and disadvantaged. This Act originally sought to protect newly freed slaves from malicious government reprisal. In its contemporary form, it is known as Title 42: Section 1983 of the U.S. Federal Code. Title 42, permits all inmates, regardless of race, to file suit for alleged abuse committed by government employees or those acting on the government's behalf. It is also the predominate Act by which inmates currently seek legal redress. Title 42, Sec. 1983 reads as follows:

Every person who, under color of any statute, ordinance, regulation, custom, or usage, of any State or Territory of the District of Columbia, subjects, or causes to be subjected, any citizen of the United States or other person within the jurisdiction thereof to the deprivation of any rights, privileges, or immunities secured by the Constitution and laws, shall be liable to the party injured in an action of law, suit in equity, or other proper proceeding for redress...

The lawsuits considered in this chapter are all Title 42: Section 1983 filings. All were filed with the federal judiciary since 1992. An extensive search was conducted to locate suits pertaining to both the private and public prison sectors. This search produced 140 private prison cases of which 108 were found to be unsuitable for further analysis. Thus, 32 private sector suits were deemed appropriate for complete analysis. Next, comparable public sector suits were located. In an attempt to be as comprehensive as possible, matching was done on a case-by-case basis regarding the court (District/Appellate) in which the suit was heard, the year the suit was filed, and the state from which the suit emerged. In every suit, the court level and the location of the suit were matched identically. On occasion it was necessary to consider a public suit that fell within a two-year time span either below or above the year of its comparable private counterpart. Once matching was complete and an adequate pool of public sector suits had been identified, suits were then randomly selected. Adequate matching was not possible on 15 public suits. Thus, 17 public sector suits were selected. Data from 49 suits form the basis for this chapter.

Each suit was analyzed with regard to its language, its imagery, and its overall presentation. Each suit was also determined as being favorable, neutral, or unfavorable toward privatization. A favorable presentation denotes an abundance of judicial comments that are complimentary to privatization. A neutral presentation denotes a balance between favorable and unfavorable judicial commentary. An unfavorable presentation denotes an abundance of judicial comments that feature negative aspects of privatization or that clearly condemn some portion of it. By limiting consideration to those statements made by federal judges, insight into prison operations is enhanced and the typical propaganda and rhetoric that is introduced by plaintiff(s) and defendant(s) are avoided. This approach is especially insightful since judicial statements represent a source of potentially unbiased and factual information. Reviews of these statements are the best method available for discovering the effects of privatization on inmates and prison operations from a purely legal standpoint.

Legal Challenges Facing the Prison

Corrections Corporation of America (CCA - a private correctional company) was named most frequently in private sector litigation followed by Wackenhut Corporation (see Table 3.1). These two private correctional companies are among the largest in operation. Similarly, the most frequently named public jurisdictions were Tennessee and Oklahoma.

In half of the suits, alleged violations of due process protections were made against the private sector, followed by allegations of inadequate medical treatment. Due process violations refer to the actions of prison operators that fall outside the scope of policy or professional mandate, or that disallow inmates an opportunity to challenge, refute, or prepare a defense against disciplinary proceedings. In contrast, a majority of the allegations made against public prisons pertained to inadequate medical treatment, followed by those related to due process protections (see Table 3.2).

41

Table 3.1   Characteristics of Private and Public Litigation

Characteristic	Private	Public
Court Level		
District	12 (37%)	4 (24%)
Appellate	20 (63%)	13 (77%)
Named in Suit		
CCA	17 (53%)	Tenn 5 (29%)
CCA/Public Entity	3 (9%)	Okla 4 (24%)
Cornell	3 (9%)	NM 3 (18%)
Capital	2 (6%)	Texas 2 (12%)
Capital/Public Entity	1 (3%)	Penn 1 (6%)
Wackenhut	1 (3%)	RI 1 (6%)
Wackenhut/Public Entity	3 (9%)	MO 1 (6%)
Unnamed/Public Entity	2 (6%)	
Legal Representation		
Attorney	8 (25%)	3 (18%)
Pro Se	23 (75%)	14 (82%)
Class Action		
Yes	3 (9%)	1 (6%)
No	29 (91%)	16 (94%)

Table 3.2   A Comparison of Alleged Violations

Alleged Violation	Private		Public		Diff*
Due Process	16	(50%)	7	(41%)	+ 9%
Medical	13	(41%)	9	(53%)	- 12%
Miscellaneous	10	(31%)**	2	(12%)***	+ 19%
Physical Security	8	(25%)	5	(29%)	- 4%
Cruel/Uns. Punishment	8	(25%)	3	(18%)	+ 7%
Religious Freedom	6	(19%)	0		+ 19%
Living Conditions	5	(16%)	2	(12%)	+ 4%
Court Access	5	(16%)	5	(30%)	- 14%
Abuse/Harassment	5	(16%)	1	(6%)	+ 10%
Physical Conditions	1	(3%)	0		+ 3%

*   Percent difference between private and public prisons.
**   Four of these were for emotional distress, three for unequal protection, and three for terrorist threats, depravation of good time credits, and non-specific civil rights violations.
***   One for failure to investigate and one for denial of access to a toilet.

The private sector experienced a greater frequency of suits alleging violations of cruel and unusual punishments, religious freedoms, living and physical conditions and abuse and harassment. A major exception is in the area of medical care where the private sector experienced a smaller percentage of allegations. This finding challenges the popular belief that medical treatment is an area ripe for financial cutbacks. Similarly, a belief that the private sector would hamper or prevent inmates' access to the judiciary to avoid financial loss is not supported by these findings. Other categories of violations and their frequencies appear in Table 3.2. A list of definitions for these categories appears at the end of this chapter.

Table 3.3 presents the number and percentage of violations pertaining to each sector. In a large majority of the private sector suits, two or more violations were claimed. Substantially fewer public sector suits involved two or more allegations. This suggests that when a suit is filed against the private sector it more frequently raises a greater number of issues than do suits filed against the public sector.

Table 3.3   Number of Allegations by Sector

Number of Allegations	Private		Public	
1	10	(31%)	8	(47%)
2	6	(19%)	4	(23%)
3	10	(31%)	2	(12%)
4	6	(19%)	3	(18%)

Judicial Views of Privatization

The following is an analysis of prison portrayals appearing in statements made by the federal judiciary. A consideration of these portrayals is essential since they are published and disseminated widely. These views influence the opinions of courts nationwide as well as those legal approaches taught within law schools. The judicial statements that follow are excerpted from suits in which issues of inmate safety, prison management, grievance processes, profit, staff training, and recreation are addressed.   With few exceptions, only excerpts of those statements that have been determined favorable or unfavorable will be reviewed since neutral statements offer little or no insight.

Safety

In a third of the private sector suits, inmate safety was a judicial concern. In approximately a tenth of these, safety was mentioned unfavorably with no favorable mention being found. Broadly defined, safety is an area that encompasses any act or practice that places inmates at risk. These risks run the gamut from simple assault to those relating to improper or untimely medical treatment, mistreatment, or non-treatment. The three private sector suits in which inmate safety was a judicial concern clearly reveal the broad and complicated nature of this subject.

In the first suit (Scott v. District of Columbia) a private prison was accepting the "most violent, assaultive and disruptive prisoners" in the region. This practice was in violation of its contractual agreement that prohibited its housing of violent offenders. The court recognized that by accepting "dangerous inmates" other inmates were placed at risk. Furthermore, this operator "failed to establish and maintain a classification system" to protect inmates from each other. Inmate classification is a process that helps identify an inmate's overall proclivity toward violence. This assessment determines which type of prison (maximum, medium, or minimum) is best suited to house a particular inmate. Furthermore, inmates with similar classifications are housed together. This is intended to ensure the safety of the less violent inmate. In this particular suit, violent and dangerous inmates were allowed to intermingle with those that were less violent and less dangerous. This resulted in the murder of a medium security inmate by an inmate that was classified maximum security. Furthermore, this maximum security inmate "had been convicted of three murders, including one committed while incarcerated." In addition to these murders, this inmate had previously stabbed a corrections officer, assaulted another corrections officer, and had seriously stabbed a fellow inmate. Yet, he was permitted to remain in general population inside a prison "designed to hold only medium-security prisoners." The Court noted that this practice clearly created an unsafe prison setting. In response, the Court stated that the government must not be permitted to abandon inmates to the private sector if aware of a significant risk to its inmates. Furthermore, the Court stated that the government can be held jointly liable if it knowingly places inmates into an unsafe setting. The Court acknowledged that the government was directly involved in creating this unsafe and deadly setting by knowingly placing inmates into a prison that failed to adequately classify or appropriately house inmates.

In the second suit (Kesler v. Brazoria County) inmates were abused and tortured by officers of a private prison. This incident prompted the court to unequivocally state that inmates "have a constitutional right to be free from excessive force." In this suit, a large group of inmates were "kicked, bitten, stunned, intrusively searched, and forced to lie naked on the floor and in their bunks for hours." When this abuse occurred inmates were compliant, with many being attacked only after laying on the floor as instructed. Plaintiffs alleged that one K-9 handler "allowed his dog to bite as many as five inmates without provocation" while others employed a stun gun against cooperative inmates. Of particular interest to the Court was the sadistic manner by which staff acted. This conduct led the Court to recognize that private operators may knowingly sacrifice inmate safety for profit. The Court stated that the:

> experience, training, and temperament [of staff] may become expendable virtues when their associated costs threaten the bottom line. The undisputed actions of CCRI [Capital Correctional Resources, Inc.] unfortunately, have done little to assuage the Court's misgivings about the privatization of prisons.

The judge presiding over this suit used the term "quack" to describe this particular private operator and "commodities" to describe the way it treated its inmates. This judge indicated that the safety and well being of these inmates came second to the prison's financial success. Accordingly, the judge perceived cost-cutting efforts (evidenced through employing low skilled individuals) as a contributing factor to this abuse. In fact, the Court likened the conduct of this operator to "cruel and unusual" punishment. For example:

> The concept of what punishments are "cruel and unusual draws it's meaning from the evolving standards of decency that marks the progress of a maturing society. When prison officials sadistically and arbitrarily employ force to harm inmates, those standards of decency are always violated.

> The Court is mindful that liability for outrageous conduct should be found only where the conduct has been so outrageous in character and so extreme in degree, as to go beyond all possible bounds of decency, and to be regarded as atrocious, and utterly intolerable in a civilized community. Indeed, in the past eight years this Court cannot remember a single claim of intentional infliction of emotional distress that it has allowed to go to a jury. However, this case presents a factual scenario this Court has not confronted before. If the facts are as Plaintiffs allege them to be, then the Court cannot recall a series of events as utterly barbaric as those now before it.

Furthermore, it clearly angered the Court that when asked about these incidents,

> each [defendant] has invoked the Fifth Amendment with respect to every single

question asked of him by Plaintiffs' counsel and offered the Court nothing more than conclusory affidavits declaring that their actions were objectively reasonable, the Court must operate within the boundaries of the incident as Plaintiffs have pictured it. We will not permit [Defendant] to invoke the Fifth Amendment to shield himself from examination while offering his self-serving statements as the only available evidence relevant to his asserted justification for the use of deadly force.

In the final suit (Bowman v. Corrections Corporation of America) similar concerns were made about the financial incentive of the private sector to jeopardize inmate safety by withholding medical treatment. This particular provider had allotted $500,000 per year to inmate medical care, yet this allotment fell far short of what was actually needed. Thus, an incentive existed for the private operator to find ways to limit and even reduce these expenditures. In this suit, an inmate with a history of sickle cell anemia was not given adequate medical attention. This inmate subsequently died. The Court observed that:

> under his contract with CCA, Dr. Coble (medical director) has significant financial incentives to limit inmate medical care. As noted by the AMA (American Medical Association), this contract creates, serious potential conflicts.

In this suit, it was revealed that staff received financial awards for limiting the amount of medical care given the inmate population. While the medical director was himself paid a salary, he could increase his pay "by $95,000 per year" by reducing medical expenditures. Such an incentive was viewed by the Court as creating a conflict of interest in which personal gain compromised inmate safety. In fact, this arrangement violated:

> contemporary standards of decency, by giving a physician who provides exclusive medical services to inmates, substantial financial incentives to double his income by reducing inmates' necessary medical services. According to the proof, Dr. Coble reached the maximum of his financial incentives for each year of his contract.

Safety was mentioned as a judicial concern in less than half of those suits filed against the public sector, and always in a neutral manner.

Prison Management and Conflict Resolution

Private prison management was mentioned unfavorably in two suits. The first suit (Kesler v. Brazoria County) concerned the abuse, harassment and assault of a large number of inmates. In this suit, a number of Missouri inmates were transferred to a private prison in Texas. While there, Missouri's inmates were to be provided "all necessities on the same basis" as other inmates. Furthermore, "all disciplinary actions were to be reasonable, proportionate and not physically abusive." A contributory factor in this case is that this particular operator knowingly hired ex-felons as correctional officers. The Court stated that:

Of the three individuals that to this Court's knowledge had prior correctional experience at the time of hiring, two turned out to be convicted criminals themselves, each in fact convicted for conduct [assault and battery] similar to that which forms the basis of this lawsuit.

Plaintiffs have produced evidence that Defendant Crawford knew of Lt. Wallace's prior conviction [for a previous incident of beating an inmate] when he applied but deliberately chose not to inquire into the specifics of the conviction.

Following an incident in which dozens of inmates were abused, more than thirty institutional grievances were filed. One investigation resulted with one officer receiving formal sanctions. Similar grievances were filed at the rate of 2 - 5 per week, but resulted in no action. While institutional policy mandated that records be maintained regarding grievances and their related investigations, only one record could be produced for the Court. This prompted the Court to recognize that there "is no evidence" that company personnel "took any actions to investigate the excessive force complaints." The Court further stated that no reasonable official (acting in a supervisory or management capacity) would believe that such deliberate indifference could be lawful. This failure to investigate:

is only exacerbated by the fact that he [the prison administrator] viewed the Missouri inmates housed in the CCRI (Capital Correctional Resources) wing of the jail as [little more than] a source of revenue.

In the second suit (Scott v. District of Columbia), the Court held that the government jurisdiction that had hired the private operator was negligent in overseeing its operation, and that the private operator was negligent in managing its facility. The plaintiff (the deceased inmate's mother) alleged that defendants "failed to comply with the recognized standards of care applicable to the management and operation of a correctional facility" by allowing a pervasively dangerous situation to persist. In this situation, the private operator allowed violent inmates to intermingle with those that were less violent. This resulted in the death of one prisoner. The court stipulated that the government should exercise reasonable care "in the selection and supervision of its independent contractors."

These two cases reinforce the judicial expectation that governmental jurisdictions be actively engaged in overseeing the management of private prisons to ensure that constitutional requisites of care are provided. In no public sector suit was prison management or mismanagement mentioned.

Methods of conflict resolution (grievances or investigations undertaken at inmate request) were mentioned in less than a quarter of the private sector suits. In no suit was it mentioned favorably, and in only one suit (Kesler v. Brazoria County) was it mentioned unfavorably. In the suit where conflict resolution was mentioned unfavorably, grievances were not physically secured and were occasionally taken by unknown inmates or staff. At other times, staff systematically discarded grievances without conducting even the most basic of investigations. The court stated:

> Fletcher's suspicions were confirmed in part when he discovered that the grievance box had been broken into at least three times. Moreover, a psychologist employed by CCRI for a brief period during 1996 and 1997 testified that she witnessed Lieutenant

51

Wallace... perfunctorily screen and discard inmate grievance forms... grievances filed in every single instance with Brazoria County officials produced no response.

Methods of conflict resolution were mentioned in 12 public sector cases and always in a neutral manner.

Profit

Profit was mentioned in slightly less than a quarter of the private sector suits with three portraying profit as having an unfavorable effect upon the prison. No suit portrayed profit's effects upon the prison as favorable. The first suit (McKnight v. Rees) involved an inmate that was restrained during transport. This inmate later claimed that the restraints caused injuries warranting hospitalization. The inmate stated that employees of this specific private prison ignored his injuries and requests for medical attention. The court stated:

> privately employed correctional officers... are not principally motivated by a desire to further the interests of the public at large. Rather, as employees of a private corporation seeking to maximize profits, correctional officers act, at least in part, out of a desire to maintain the profitability of the corporation... for profit corporations - and indirectly the employees of those corporations - seek to realize what the name implies, a profit. Accordingly, private corporations running correctional facilities have a greater incentive to cut costs by infringing upon the

constitutional rights of prisoners in order to ensure the profitability of the enterprise.

the balance struck by qualified immunity, at least implicitly, contemplates a government actor acting for the good of the state, not a private actor acting for the good of the pocketbook. With respect to cutting corners on constitutional guarantees, one commentator has explained that entrepreneurial jailers benefit directly, in the form of increased profits, from every dime not spent.

In the second suit (Bowman v. Corrections Corporation of America) the Plaintiff's mother won her case when the court found that CCA had denied her son proper medical care as a way to decrease expenditures and increase profit. The court awarded the plaintiff $46,877.85. Furthermore, the Court stated that:

Plaintiff has presented evidence that Defendant CCA, in carrying out its contract with the State of Tennessee, increases its profits if it keeps its actual costs down. Thus, CCA also has financial incentive to reduce medical costs at South Central Correctional Center. Plaintiff contends that CCA had adopted a policy of providing a financial incentive to its contract physicians to deny or delay medical care to prison inmates in order to increase the physician's income and also CCA's profits.

In the final suit (Kesler v. Brazoria County) the private operator ran a 512-bed facility. This prison was projected to produce a profit in excess of $2 million over a three-year period. This endeavor was described by the prison's administrator as a "money-maker." In its review, the Court used the terms "quack" to describe this particular private prison and "inmate commodities" to describe the manner by which its inmates were perceived. These statements left little doubt about the Court's perception of Capital Correctional Resources Incorporated. The Court made it quite clear that in its estimation, this operator had failed to train its officers, employ quality personnel, supervise its employees, or even investigate inmate grievances, all as a means to increase profit margins. The court further stated that:

> The injection of profit seeking into the prison environment complicates this inherent difficulty [of overseeing and working within a jail or prison]. Experience, training, and temperament may become expendable virtues when their associated costs threaten the bottom line. Although such corporations potentially could help alleviate the very real problems of overcrowding in the federal and state prison systems, they are still in the business of making a profit.

In one private sector suit where profit was mentioned neutrally (Citrano v. Allen Correctional Center), the court questioned the feasibility of squeezing profit from cost cutting measures that would, in all probability, result in civil judgments. In the Court's estimation such an endeavor would prove difficult at best.

Profit was mentioned in one public sector suit (neutrally) when the Court entertained an allegation that civil rights had been violated because the defendant misused state funds for his "own financial and political gain." The suit (West

v. Keating) was summarily dismissed.

Employee Training

Employee training was mentioned in slightly more than a tenth of the private sector suits. All but one portrayed employee training neutrally. In Kesler v. Brazoria County, where training was mentioned unfavorably, it was claimed that inmate abuses were due, in part, to the private operator's "failure to train and supervise" its staff. The Court recognized that:

> at least one CCRI officer conducted several [such] searches despite the fact that he had received no training in how to conduct a strip search. In fact, this officer had received no training at all in law enforcement.

> the only training that [these] personnel had received was in opening and closing cellblock doors.

> the Court is satisfied that the violent and humiliating events of that evening were substantially and causally related to the lack of training and supervision.

No public sector suit mentioned staff training.

Recreation

It has been suggested that inmate recreation is an area ripe for budgetary cutbacks. Public concern has long persisted about providing inmates with sport and recreational equipment that exceeds what is available to most citizens. Furthermore, recreational equipment is expensive and through constant use and sometimes abuse, needs to be replaced frequently. Therefore, the purchase and repurchase of equipment is a constant drain on prison budgets. Knowing that inmates take recreational activities seriously, one would expect to see a high number of related complaints being filed with the judiciary if cutbacks have been instituted sector-wide. However, no mention was made of recreational activity in litigation filed against the private sector. Furthermore, only one public sector suit mentioned recreation. This mention was neutral in context and was little more than a brief reference with regard to the placement of an inmate into restrictive housing. The inmate admitted that this placement was for an incident in which he was later charged and found guilty of "disrespect to staff or citizen." The inmate claimed that he was maliciously denied recreational activity (for one day) without due process (Bridgeforth v. Ramsey). The Court replied that the alleged deprivations were "not sufficiently grave to warrant relief" and did not deprive the inmate of "life's necessities."

Private and Public Comparisons

In approximately 10 percent of the private sector suits, comparisons were made between the sectors. In the first suit, private employees were compared to their public counterparts, with the Court suggesting that each have similar responsibilities (Citrano v. Allen Correctional Center). For example, when considering whether private staff should be given the legal immunities enjoyed by public officials, the Court stated:

> The prison guards and correctional officers at
> Allen Correctional Center [ACC] are required
> to perform the same functions and are faced

with the same types of situations requiring the exercise of discretion as are state employees working in state prisons. The only difference is that those working at ACC do so pursuant to an employment contract with a state contractor whereas state employees do so pursuant to an employment contract with the state. They [private sector employees] are the functional equivalent of state prison employees.

Thus, this Court clearly saw no difference between the public officer and his/her private counterpart. Such a determination was based largely upon an examination of the functional duties that each performs.

In the second suit (Kesler v. Brazoria Country) the Court recognized that many of the challenges facing the prison make it a difficult place to work. In fact, the prison is by its "very nature [an] involuntary destination for persons who have a demonstrated proclivity for anti-social, and often violent, conduct." However, the Court indicated that "the injection of profit-seeking" into this environment complicates its very nature. In fact, the private sector's pursuit of profit makes it more likely to reduce the amount and quality of employee training. Thus, the Court saw a clear distinction between the sectors, with the pursuit of profit being the defining feature of the private sector.

In the final case (McKnight v. Rees), the Court compared private and public correctional officers. In this comparison, the Court stated numerous times that those employed by each sector have inherently different interests. It is these "different interests" that the Court believes disqualifies the private sector from many of the legal immunities enjoyed by its public counterparts. The Court viewed the private sector's primary objectives as being profit and self-perpetuation, whereas the objective of the public sector is the promotion of the public's interests. "Private parties hold no office requiring them to exercise discretion, nor are they principally concerned with enhancing the public good."

In no suit filed against the public sector were its prisons compared to those of the private sector.

Summary

The overall context of privatization as presented in private sector litigation was neutral in 28 suits, favorable in one (Citrano v. Allen Correctional Center) and unfavorable in three (Bowman v. CCA; Kesler v. Brazoria County; McKnight v. Rees). In all public sector suits, public prisons were presented in a neutral context. Little definitive evidence has been found to suggest that suits filed against the private sector are more frequently linked to profit and efficiency that are suits filed against the public sector. This determination is based upon a consideration of those categories of violations that can be practically linked to a financial motive, including medical treatment, physical security, and living and physical conditions. In both the medical and physical security categories, the private sector experienced a smaller percentage of suits alleging violations than did the public sector. In the living and physical conditions categories, the private sector experienced a greater percentage of alleged violations. Therefore, based solely upon a consideration of these four categories of violations, no determination can be made about the potential effects of profit. However, in the small number of suits where issues of profit were central, judicial statements implied that the private sector is more likely than the public sector to infringe upon inmate civil rights. Furthermore, judicial statements made in response to suits filed against the private sector carried greater levels of admonishment than those directed toward the public sector. These statements were more stern and corrective in nature. Judicial comments send a clear message that according to a portion of the federal judiciary, private operators act or potentially act in a manner deserving of examination and vigilance. Thus, when considering alleged violations and their related judicial statements, it clearly appears that the private sector is nearer the less eligibility end of the ideological continuum than is the public sector. Furthermore, by comparing the private to the publicly operated prison, the Court promotes the position that public prisons adhere to standards that the private sector, as a whole, does not. This perspective largely ignores the reality that the public sector has had its share of litigation pertaining to civil rights infringements. It is also clear that a portion of the federal judiciary considers privately held inmates to be at risk for commodification (Bowman v. CCA; Kesler v. Brazoria County; McKnight v. Rees; Grams v. Kaiser) and that private operators have an inherent incentive to withhold or reduce a wide range of inmate services. Judicial statements also suggest that the private sector may hire less qualified staff, provide less training, and hire fewer employees as a means to increase profit margins.

Discussion Questions

1).   Why do judicial statements made to the private sector tend to carry greater levels of admonishment and appear to be more corrective in nature than statements made to public prison operators?

2).   Why is it important for the inmate population to have access to the judiciary? Should limitations be placed upon this access?   If so, what limitations do you propose?

3).   Why does the judiciary require that government jurisdictions monitor the actions and services of its private operators? If a government jurisdiction fails to monitor the actions of its private operator(s) should it be held jointly liable for any unconstitutional action that occurs? Why?

Cases Reviewed

Adkins v. Cooper et al., United States Court of Appeals
for the Ninth Circuit (No. 00-15897) (LEXIS 5319);
Filed March 26, 2001.

Barkus v. Kaiser et al., United States Court of Appeals
for the Tenth Circuit (No. 00-7044) (Lexis 23638);
Filed September 19, 2000.

Baxter v. Williams et al., United States Court of Appeals
for the Tenth Circuit (No. 01-2142) (LEXIS 1882);
Filed February 6, 2002.

Billings v. CCA et al., United States Court of Appeals
for the Tenth Circuit (No. 99-6186) (LEXIS 137); Filed
January 6, 2000.

Boulden v. Tafoya et al., United States Court of Appeals
for the Tenth Circuit (No. 02-2024) (LEXIS 12351);
Filed June 21, 2002.

Bowman v. Correction Corporation America et al.,
United States District Court for the Middle District of
Tennessee, Nashville Division (No. 3:96-1142) (LEXIS
21898); Entered March 15, 2000.

Bridgeforth v. Ramsey et al., United States Court of Appeals
for the Tenth Circuit (No. 99-6179) (LEXIS 28886);
Filed November 2, 1999.

Carillo v. Dubois, United States District Court for the
District of Massachusetts (No. 97-10468-RCL)
(LEXIS 14595); Decided September 10, 1998.

Citrano and Chapman v. Allen Correctional Center,
United States District Court for the Western District of
Louisiana, Lake Charles Division (CV 94-1076) (LEXIS
8598); June 14, 1995.

Duarte-Vestar v. Hudson et al., United States Court of
Appeals for the Tenth Circuit (No. 99-6423) (LEXIS
11803); Filed May 26, 2000.

Farrell v. Addison et al., United States Court of Appeals
for the Tenth Circuit (No. 01-7094, No. 01-7127)
(LEXIS 7101); Filed April 17, 2002.

Frazier v. Johnson et al., United States Court of Appeals
for the Tenth Circuit (No. 01-2323) (LEXIS 7612);
Filed April 25, 2002.

Friedman v. CCA et al., United States Court of Appeals
for the Sixth Circuit (No. 99-6587) (LEXIS 8107); Filed
April 26, 2001.

Giron v. Corrections Corporation of America et al., U.S.
District Court for the District of New Mexico (No 96-
0980 LH/DJS) (LEXIS 18643): Filed July 2, 1998 and
U.S. Court of Appeals for the Tenth Circuit (No. 98-
2231) (LEXIS 18643): Filed September 10, 1999.

Grams v. Kaiser, Warden of CCA-Davis et al., United
States Court of Appeals for the Tenth Circuit (No. 00-
7101) (LEXIS 5771); Filed April 6, 2001.

Green v. Corrections Corporation of America, United
States Court of Appeals for the Sixth Circuit (No. 98-
6573) (LEXIS 29983); Filed November 10, 1999.

Grundy v. Norris, Director of the Arkansas Department of Corrections et al., United States Court of Appeals for the Eighth Circuit (No. 01-1855) (LEXIS 23716); Filed November 2, 2001.

Hogan v. Oklahoma Department of Corrections et al., United States Court of Appeals for the Tenth Circuit (No. 98-6127) (LEXIS 2896); Filed February 22, 1999.

Horton v. CCA et al., United States Court of Appeals for the Sixth Circuit (No. 98-5878) (LEXIS 22496); Filed August 11, 1999.

Johnson v. Bowlen et al., United States Court of Appeals for the Sixth Circuit (No. 99-6066) (LEXIS 19213); Filed August 8, 2000.

Kesler et al., v. Brazoria County Sheriff King et al., United States District Court for the Southern District of Texas, Galveston Division (No. G-96-703)(LEXIS 19282); Entered December 7, 1998.

Kirk v. Capital Services et al., United States Court of Appeals for the Tenth Circuit (No. 99-6178) (LEXIS 2347); Filed February 16, 2000.

Lawson v. Liburdi et al., United States District Court for the District of Rhode Island (C.A. No. 98-533 ML); Filed August 23, 2000.

Leslie et al., v. Wisconsin Department of Corrections, United States Court of Appeals for the Seventh Circuit (No. 99-2034) (Lexis 11850); Entered May 24, 2000.

Lewis v. Aramark Service, CCA et al., United States Court of Appeals for the Sixth Circuit (No. 003601) (LEXIS 33230); Filed December 8, 2000.

Jones v. Barry et al., United States Court of Appeals for the Tenth Circuit (No. 01-2092) (LEXIS 7620); Filed April 25, 2002.

Martin v. Capital Services et al., United States Court of Appeals for the Tenth Circuit (No. 99-6171) (LEXIS 2346); Filed February 16, 2000.

McKnight v. Rees et al., U.S. Court of Appeals for the Sixth Circuit (No. 95-5398) (LEXIS 16385); Filed July 10, 1996.

Montgomery v. Kaiser et al., United States Court of Appeals for the Tenth Circuit (No. 99-7099) (LEXIS 6722); Filed April 12, 2000.

Nolan v. Martin et al., United States Court of Appeals for the Tenth Circuit (No. 98-6443) (LEXIS 18189); Filed August 3, 1999.

Oliver v. Scott et al., U.S. District Court for the Northern District of Texas, Dallas Division (No. 3:98-CV-22 46-H) (LEXIS 1620); Filed February 4, 2000.

Perry v. Rose et al., U.S. Court of Appeals for the Sixth Circuit (No. 99-5240) (LEXIS 1918); Filed February 7, 2000.

Poareo v. Johnson et al., United States Court of Appeals for the Tenth Circuit (No. 02-2136) (LEXIS 17907); Filed August 29, 2002.

Rainey v. County of Delaware, United States District Court for the Eastern District of Pennsylvania (No. 00-548) (LEXIS 10700); Filed August 1, 2000.

Ratliff v. Fields et al., United States Court of Appeals for the
Tenth Circuit (No. 98-7119) (LEXIS 12045); Filed June
11, 1999.

Russell v. Casey et al., United States Court of Appeals for the
Sixth Circuit (No. 98-5348) (LEXIS 19794); Filed
August 16, 1999.

Sarro, III v. The Donald Wyatt Detention Center et al.,
United States District Court for the District of Rhode
Island (C.A. No. 00-011 T) (LEXIS 2375); Filed
January 30, 2001.

Scott v. District of Columbia et al., United States District
Court for the District of Columbia (98-01645(HHK))
(LEXIS 21616); Filed November 22, 1999.

Smith v. CCA, et al., United States Court of Appeals for the
Sixth Circuit (No. 00-5521) (LEXIS 3582); Filed
February 28, 2001.

Smith v. Stubblefield et al., United States District Court for
the Eastern District of Missouri, Eastern District (No.
4:98-CV-89 CAS) (LEXIS 19521); Decided November
2, 1998.

Sotherland v. Myers et al., United States Court of Appeals for
the Sixth Circuit (No. 01-6438) (LEXIS 12869); Filed
June 25, 2002.

Stanely v. Lucero et al., United States Court of Appeals for the
Tenth Circuit (No. 01-2204) (LEXIS 15867); Filed
August 7, 2002.

Thomas v. Dragovich et al., United States District Court for
the Eastern District of Pennsylvania (No. 97-5814)
(LEXIS 4761); Filed March 28, 2000.

Tidline v. Franklin et al., United States District Court for the Northern District of Texas, Lubbock Division (No. 5: 99-CV-321-C) (Lexis 18298); Filed November 8, 2001.

Treat v. CCA et al., United States Court of Appeals for the Sixth Circuit (No. 00-6000) (LEXIS 14014); Filed June 18, 2001.

West v. Keating, United States Court of Appeals for the Tenth Circuit (No. 00-7129) (LEXIS 18339); Filed August 13, 2001.

Wilson v. Reynolds et al., United States Court of Appeals for the Sixth Circuit (No. 97-5566) (LEXIS 31355); Filed December 10, 1998.

Witty v. Simpson et al., United States District Court for the Northern District of Texas, Dallas Division (3:01-CV-0005-R) (LEXIS 3987); Filed January 22, 2001.

York v. Mills et al., United States Court of Appeals for the Sixth Circuit (No. 99-5391) (LEXIS 4879); Filed March 17, 2000.

Definitions of Violations Filed Under
Title 42: Section 1983

(1)   Medical treatment (failure to provide back brace, corrective shoes, dentures, or failure to perform necessary surgery).

(2)   Physical security (excessive force by staff, failure to protect against attacks and rapes, failure to prevent theft of property, unreasonable/unlawful searches, wrongful death, negligent supervision).

(3)   Due process (improper placement/non-placement into administrative segregation, improper intra-prison transfer, improper disciplinary hearing, improper classification, denial of speech or mail confiscation).

(4)   Living conditions (nutritionally inadequate diet, denial or extreme limitation of exercise or inadequate clothing).

(5)   Physical conditions (overcrowding inadequate toilets and showers, excessive noise, inadequate sanitation).

(6)   Denial or religious freedoms (denial of religious expression, assembly or worship).

(7)   Denial of access to appropriate courts, law libraries, and lawyers.

(8)   Abuse, harassment, or assault by correctional staff (taunting, threatening, name calling, or touching not called for by circumstance).

(9)   Cruel and unusual punishment often cited in conjunction with the 8th Amendment. This allegation is usually made in conjunction with one of the previous allegations (1-8). This category refers to actions that shock the conscience of the average citizen and exceed ideals of fair and humane treatment.

(10)   Miscellaneous is a category reserved for unusual or unforeseen allegations that do not readily fit into one of the previous categories.

Adapted from: Hanson and Daley, 1994. *Challenging the conditions of prisons and jails: A report on section 1983 litigation.* A BJS Discussion Paper 92 BJ-CX-K026.

CHAPTER 4

Privatization and the Print Media

Newspaper accounts reveal a great deal about how the print media perceives and portrays prison privatization. A greater understanding of these perceptions and their subsequent portrayals is beneficial since the print media is largely responsible for informing the public about prison-related issues. In fact, it has been observed that the print media effectively influences the views and opinions of over half the U.S. adults (Dizard, 2000; Graber, 1980). Since most individuals are unfamiliar with prison privatization, they rely upon the print media for the information that they will, in turn, use to form personal opinions and viewpoints. These opinions and viewpoints, taken in their entirety, help determine the degree of support given prison privatization by the public.

To accomplish the specific objective of this chapter, ProQuest, a computerized information retrieval service used by academic and research institutions worldwide was used to locate newspaper articles in which the term "private prison" appeared. The use of ProQuest was deemed particularly appropriate since it allows searches to be conducted as far back as 1986, the approximate year of privatization's re-emergence. A search was conducted for each year beginning January 1, 1986 and ending on April 18, 2002. This search revealed that 2,654 articles were fully accessible. For the years of 1986 to 1989, few articles existed; thus, articles appearing in the 1980s were randomly sampled at 15 percent. For the years of 1990 to 2002, a greater number of articles were located. Because a greater number of articles exist within this time frame, 5 percent of these articles were randomly selected. Collectively, this resulted in the selection of 151 articles. After preliminary analysis, 22 articles were discarded because they were unrelated to prison privatization or contained little more than a contextual reference. After discarding these 22 articles, 129 were determined suitable for complete analysis. Table 4.1 provides the frequency of articles by year.

Table 4.1   Frequency of Articles by Year

Year	Number of Articles Available in Full Text
2002	107
2001	192
2000	282
1999	503
1998	498
1997	363
1996	259
1995	184
1994	33
1993	64
1992	34
1991	47
1990	24
1989	9
1988	11
1987	30
1986	14

Tables 4.2 and 4.3 depict a number of widely read newspapers and the frequency of privatization-related articles that each published per year. For ease of arrangement, articles are classified as appearing in southern or non-southern newspapers. This was done since a majority of private prisons are located in southern states. The frequency of articles was more prevalent in the south with the *Albuquerque Journal* publishing 185 articles since 1986. Of the non-southern

70

newspapers, the *Washington Post* published the greatest number of articles, 41 since 1986.

Table 4.2   Frequency of Articles by Newspaper and Region (South)

Year	Houston Chronicle	Nashville Banner	Albuquerque Journal	Atlanta Journal
2002	1	0	0	0
2001	4	0	11	0
2000	0	0	45	1
1999	10	0	79	6
1998	2	4	24	8
1997	9	13	11	2
1996	17	1	15	5
1995	1	2	0	1
1994	1	0	0	0
1993	10	0	0	0
1992	4	0	0	0
1991	6	0	0	0
1990	9	0	0	0
1989	2	0	0	0
1988	6	0	0	0
1987	17	0	0	0
1986	0	0	0	0
TOTAL	**99**	**20**	**185**	**23**

Table 4.3 Frequency of Articles by Newspaper and Region (Non-South)

Year	Washington Post	Boston Herald	NY Times	Chicago Tribune	LA Times
2002	1	0	2	0	5
2001	8	2	2	1	2
2000	3	0	1	1	0
1999	7	0	2	0	7
1998	11	0	0	3	2
1997	2	0	6	2	2
1996	1	0	0	0	2
1995	2	0	3	1	0
1994	0	1	1	0	2
1993	0	0	0	0	1
1992	2	0	0	0	1
1991	3	0	0	1	6
1990	0	0	0	2	0
1989	0	0	1	0	1
1988	1	0	0	0	2
1987	0	0	0	0	1
1986	0	0	0	0	3
TOTAL	**41**	**3**	**18**	**11**	**37**

Once selected, the content of the articles were analyzed. This analysis included a consideration of the topics of safety, recreation, prison management, conflict resolution, institutional capacity, civil rights issues, and staff. The language used in each article and the manner by which prisons were generally portrayed was also determined as being favorable, neutral, or unfavorable. A favorable presentation refers to those articles or issues that are complimentary to privatization. A neutral presentation refers to those articles or issues that are neither favorable nor unfavorable or whose presentation is generally balanced. An unfavorable presentation refers to those articles or issues that feature a negative aspect of privatization or portrays privatization as a negative social phenomenon.

Newspaper articles used within this chapter represent 22 states, the District of Columbia, and the United Kingdom. Fifty-seven percent of these articles are from a non-southern state while 43 percent originated in the south (AZ, NM, OK, TX, AL, AR, FL, GA, KY, LA, MS, NC, SC, TN, VA, WV). The company most frequently identified within these articles was Corrections Corporation of America (CCA). CCA was named in 38 percent of the articles. In 11 percent of these, CCA was identified along with at least one additional company. Wackenhut Corporation was identified in 17 percent of the articles, with 9 percent of these naming Wackenhut along with at least one additional company. In 6 percent of the articles, both CCA and Wackenhut were jointly named.

Article Titles

A pattern emerged with regard to the overall nature of article titles. During the 1980s, titles were unfavorable in a third of the articles, neutral in half, and favorable in approximately 17 percent. During the 1990s, approximately one-third of the titles were unfavorable, with 64 percent being neutral and 6 percent being favorable. During 2000-2002, 35 percent of the titles were unfavorable, with 62 percent being neutral and 4 percent being favorable. Thus, article titles have become less favorable and more neutral with the percentage of unfavorable titles remaining relatively unchanged since 1986 (see Table 4.4 for trends).

A sample of unfavorable, neutral, and favorable titles include the following:

Unfavorable

Prisons run for profit may turn out not to be all that profitable (*The Santa Fe New Mexican,* 1996).

Private prisons scoff at Fla. law (*Palm Beach Post,* 1997).

State inmates in private prison file suit: Federal lawsuits allege guards tortured, violated civil rights of Wisconsin prisoners in Tennessee (*Milwaukee Journal Sentinel,* 1999).

Neutral

1st private prison planned for Santa Clarita (*Los Angeles Times,* 1988).

Prison firms to merge in $2.9 billion deal (*Los Angeles Times,* 1998).

Private prison is suggested for those who drink, drive (*Omaha World Herald,* 1998).

Favorable

D.C. looks at prisons run for profit: private facilities may ease crowding (*The Washington Post,* 1988).

Town profits from prison (*The Plain Dealer*, 1995).

Utah's Wendover willing to bet on private prison: Wendover wants private prison to rescue economy (*The Salt Lake Tribune*, 1999).

Titles that were unfavorable tended to use language that portrayed privatization as a practice that abuses inmates, infringes on civil rights and operates without restriction. In an opposite fashion, favorable titles tended to focus upon the financial and economic benefits of privatization including the creation of jobs.

Article Content

When considering article content by decade, during the 1980s, 25 percent of the content was unfavorable, 58 percent was neutral, and 17 percent favorable. During the 1990s, 37 percent was unfavorable, 56 percent neutral, and approximately 7 percent favorable. During the 2000s, 46 percent of the content was unfavorable, 46 percent neutral, and approximately 8 percent favorable. Thus, the biggest difference in article content was in the unfavorable category where the percentage of unfavorable content has nearly doubled. A sample of unfavorable, neutral, and favorable article excerpts include:

Unfavorable

Two former executives of a company that will build North Carolina's first private prisons are in prison or under indictment on federal corruption charges (*Greensboro News Record*, 1996).

CCA fired seven employees, including the security chief at the prison last fall when then Wisconsin Corrections Secretary Michael Sullivan found evidence of inmate abuse, complained of a CCA cover-up and asked the FBI to investigate (*Wisconsin State Journal*, 1999).

The privatization experiment was marred by problems that included riots, and other violence, abusive and untrained officers, plus inadequate medical care, educational programs and rehabilitation (*Advocate*, 2000).

Neutral

California has been experimenting with privately run correctional centers since the 1980s. One dozen facilities that cater to nonviolent offenders now operate in the state (*Los Angeles Times*, 1996).

About 30 percent of New Mexico's 4,724 inmates are held in private prisons (*Albuquerque Journal*, 1999).

Favorable

> I think it ought to be tried, said
> Hobby (Lt. Governor of Texas).
> Apparently, they've (private prison
> operators) had a good record in other
> states (*Houston Chronicle*, 1987).

> But inmates say privatization already
> has succeeded in other ways: The
> facility is cleaner and has better food
> and more humane conditions than any
> state prison they have experienced
> (*Austin American Statesman*, 1989).

These excerpts reveal the general nature of unfavorable statements and their portrayal of privatization as a practice that is largely void of public accountability and in need of government restriction. References to inmate beatings, political corruption, and external investigations were frequent. Furthermore, profit was frequently mentioned in conjunction with a reduction or elimination of inmate services. When considering favorable statements, references to the private sector's past successes and current facility conditions were common. Patterns related to title and article content are depicted on Table 4.4.

**Table 4.4   Article Title and Content: January 1, 1986 -
April 18, 2002**

Decade	Unfavorable	Neutral	Favorable
80's			
Title	33% (4)*	50% (6)	17% (2)
Content	25% (3)	58% (7)	17% (2)
90's			
Title	30% (29)	63% (58)	6% (5)
Content	37% (34)	56% (51)	7% (6)
2000's			
Title	35% (9)	61% (16)	4% (1)
Content	46% (12)	46% (12)	8% (2)

* Percent and number of articles by category

Keyword and Topic Analysis

A search for specific keywords and topics was
also conducted. Keywords and topics were counted, with their
usage determined as being unfavorable, neutral, or favorable
(see Table 4.5).

Table 4.5 Keywords and Topics Pertaining to Prison Privatization

	Number/Percentage of articles	% of times mentioned F*	N*	U*
PRISONS				
Capacity Level	79 (62%)	6%	79%	15%
Crowding/Overcrowding	31 (24)	7	74	19
Prison Conditions	42 (33)	5	17	62
Profit	32 (25)	3	53	44
Save/Savings	27 (20)	33	56	11
Efficient/Efficiency	15 (12)	53	33	13
Profit's effects on civil rights	6 (5)	----	17	83
Violent/Violence	31 (24)	3	58	39
Safe/Unsafe	15 (12)	13	53	33
STAFF				
Prison Admn./Operation	29 (23)	10	24	62
Suit/Suing/Lawsuit/Liability	27 (21)	----	74	26
Corrupt/Corruption	3 (2)	----	----	2
Wages	19 (15)	37	5	58
Training	11 (9)	-----	36	64
Turnover	9 (7)	----	----	100
INMATE				
Treatment/Training	21 (16)	19	62	----
Grievance/Conflict Reso.	13 (10)	----	85	15
Inmate Labor	9 (7)	22	33	22
Inmate Discipline	4 (3)	----	25	75
Due Process	4 (3)	----	50	50
Recreation	7 (5)	----	57	43

* F=Favorable; N= Neutral; U=Unfavorable

Prison capacity levels were mentioned in 62% of the articles with the words crowding or overcrowding appearing in 24 percent of the articles. Most of these references pertained to the private sector's ability to provide needed space. Conditions associated with private confinement were mentioned in approximately a third of the articles with a majority of these being unfavorable. The topic of private sector administration appeared in 23 percent of the articles with a majority of these being unfavorable. Likewise, the topic of private sector wages appeared in 15 percent of the articles with most portraying its wages as much lower than the public sector's. Furthermore, it was occasionally implied that low wages make it difficult for the private sector to attract and retain quality staff.

Private and Public Sector Comparisons

In 31 percent of the articles the private and public sectors were compared. Twenty-five percent of these pertained to financial matters. This topic was the largest single area of comparison. Other areas included institutional violence and escape levels. Comparative statements include:

> Currently, it costs $78 a day to house prisoners in state-run prisons. Johnson (Governor of New Mexico) said the private prison contractors have offered to house prisoners at $46 a day with no loss of programs for inmates (*The Santa Fe New Mexican*, 1997).

> Private prisons have come under fire in New Mexico because of a riot earlier this month at the private jail in Torrance County and because of four killings since December at the private prisons in Hobbs and Santa Rosa. So far this year, there has been one slaying at a state-run prison (*Albuquerque Journal*, 1999).

> Across the nation, men and women work in potentially life-threatening situations in our jails and prisons. Obviously they are compensated, but in the public prisons they serve at the pleasure of the taxpayers, and they are directly accountable to the public.

80

No so in private prisons (*The Washington Post*, 1999).

The prison service's bid (England's Federalized Correctional Department) was judged 18% better on quality and 20% cheaper on costs than the nearest private company (*The Guardian*, 2001).

Many comparisons suggested that the private sector is inherently more efficient than the public sector. Other comparisons suggested that private sector prisons are generally more dangerous and less secure.

Summary

The print media overwhelmingly portrays prison privatization as a financial issue. In approximately a third of the articles, comparisons were made with regard to financial matters. The print media largely ignored the role played by profit in civil rights issues and the potential for profit to become the dominant goal of the private sector. For example, the traditional penal objectives of punishment and rehabilitation were mentioned in only one article; whereas, profit and financial issues dominated title and article content. By linking incarceration to finances and by ignoring it as a practice grounded in punishment and reform ideologies, the private prison is depicted as little more than an efficient human warehouse. Furthermore, the print media also focused a majority of its attention on privatization's external characteristics and ignored those characteristics more internally situated. Therefore, the subjects of economic benefits and political processes generally preempted those issues more intimately related to inmates, staff, and correctional ideologies.

The reason for this is unknown, however, it may be the result of an inability by the print media to access the internal workings of the private prison. Such an inability has repeatedly been expressed within the literature.

Article titles and content are becoming less favorable and more neutral, with the percentage of unfavorable content nearly doubling since 1986. As such, the private sector is currently being portrayed more negatively now than at any previous time. The factors responsible for this trend are unknown, however, given the proliferation in the number of private prison operators and the increased scrutiny given the contemporary prison by politicians, labor unions and academicians, a more critical approach is not entirely unexpected. Overall, the print media portrays the private prison sector as being much more oriented toward the ideology of less eligibility than is the public sector.

Discussion Questions

1). What factors may account for the increasingly critical approach given prison privatization by the print media?

2). Why does the print media tend to focus on the private sector's financial characteristics rather than upon those characteristics that are more internally situated? Could this be a result of the private sector's refusal to allow the media access to its internal operations? Could such a refusal explain, in part, the increased amount of criticism given privatization by the print media?

Sources

Dizard, Wilson, 2000. *Old media, new media: Mass communications in the information age* (3rd. edition). New York, Longman.

Graber, D.A., 1980. *Crime news and the public.* New York: Praeger.

Newspapers Reviewed

Advocate, (May 21, 2000). *Private prisons, state obligation.* Baton Rouge, La.; Pp. 10-B.

Albuquerque Journal, (August 22, 1996). *Better-designed prisons could cut state's costs* by Peter Eichstaedt. Pp. A1.

Albuquerque Journal, (September 11, 1996). *Tough prisons backed* by Peter Eichstaedt. Pp. 1.

Albuquerque Journal, (February 18, 1998). *Deal to buy prisons stinks* by Jerry Alwin. Pp. A9.

Albuquerque Journal, (September 1, 1998). *Prison doors slam shut on old main* by Loie Fedteau. Pp. C3.

Albuquerque Journal, (August 31, 1999). *Prison violence trends examined* by Loie Fedteau, Pp. C-1.

Albuquerque Journal, (September 18, 1999). *Officials ok one prison probe* by Michael Coleman. Pp. A1.

Albuquerque Journal, (January 18, 2000). *Olguin quits dem party position* by Michael Coleman. Pp. C3.

Albuquerque Journal, (March 29, 2000). *Commission given green light to immigrant jail* by Dale Lezon. Pp. 1.

Anchorage Daily News, (May 5, 1996). *Private prison bonds now share same fate both anchorage facility, debt must pass* by Jim Clarke. Pp B1.

Anchorage Daily News, (February 4, 1998). *Town takes a long look at prison bid* by Natalie Phillips. Pp. A1.

Arizona Daily Star, (March 11, 1999). *Prison-bound biker run alarms Sun City vistoso folks* by Carmen Duarte. Pp. 1B.

Atlanta Constitution, (July 6, 1998). *Despite problems in other states, Georgia plans 3 private prisons* by Rhonda Cook. Pp. C1.

Atlanta Journal, (February 1996). *Editorials 1996 Georgia legislative session let state run its prisons.*

Atlanta Journal, (August 15, 1998). *Sheriff may sue over jail crowding; Legislature, governor warned: Georgia prison faces crunch* by Rhonda Cook. Pp. D1.

Augusta Chronicle, (March 24, 1999). *Prison hospital has shortage of patients.* Pp. C11.

Augusta Chronicle, (March 7, 2001). *Prisons bill passes in house* by Doug Gross. Pp. C12.

Austin American Statesman, (December 17, 1989). *The promise of private prisons//Kyle facility shoots for quality* by Henry Krausse, Pp. B1.

Austin American Statesman, (January 25, 1997). *Inmate with short time left to serve in prison flees from Lockhart facility.* Pp. B2.

Austin American Statesman, (August 27, 1997). *Corrections system is no place for profit* by Richard Moran. Pp. A17.

Austin American Statesman, (September 26, 1997). *Officials won't rush new rules on jails* by Mike Ward. Pp. B1.

Billings Gazette, (January 10, 1997). *Ban on importing cons rejected* by Kathleen McLaughlin. Pp. C1.

Boston Globe, (June 24, 1997). *Court: No legal immunity for private prison guards.* Pp. A13.

Commercial Appeal, (April 12, 1995). *Briggs faults prison bid.* Pp A13.

Commercial Appeal, (March 30, 2001). *Senate overrides veto of prisons budget.* Pp. DS1.

Commercial Appeal, (June 21, 1999). *Mason mayor sees no conflict in CCA prison transactions* by Marc Perrusquia. Pp. A5.

Commercial Appeal, (December 6, 2001). *Space opens at CCA private prison; But lawmakers balk at talk of using facility.* Pp. B1.

Daily News, (July 4, 1999). *Prison problems unlocked* by Jim Skeen. Pp. AV1.

Daily Record, (September 17, 2001). *Private prison No2 McLeish is set to give the go-ahead* by Magnus Gardham. Pp. 17.

Dayton Daily News, (July 27, 1998). *Youngstown; 3 more escapees in custody* by M.R. Kropko. Pp. 2B.

Denver Post, (October 2, 1990). *Aurora council members cool to pre-parole prison facility* by Renate Robey. Pp. 2B.

Denver Post, (March 14, 1997). *Plan to build prison in Wiggins withdrawn* by Coleman Cornelius. Pp. B1.

Denver Post, (January 1998). *Colorado withdraws rest of its inmates from Texas* by Steve Lipsher. Pp. B3.

Denver Rocky Mountain News, (September 30, 1999). *Private prison hired felon as guard staffer - Inmate affairs are under investigation at Burlington lockup* by Carla Crowder. Pp. 7a.

Denver Rocky Mountain News, (July 24, 1999). Burlington *prison officials phase out lockdown* by Joe Garner. Pp. 7a.

Evening News, (April 17, 2002). *Union may fund SNP in prison protest.* Pp. 9.

Evening Times, (April 23, 2001). *Private jail firm's refugee centre bid.* Pp. 2.

Evening Times, (April 24, 2002). *Prison officers call for rethink.* Pp. 15.

Florida Times Union, (November 6, 1996). *Legal system lags behind private prison industry.* Pp. A6.

Greensboro News Record, (July 10, 1996). *Former prison builders face own legal problems,* Pp. B2.

Guardian, (October 18, 1993). *Jail riot report warning for Howard* by Alan Travis.

Guardian, (January 23, 1995). *Opponents of private prison may get kicked into touch* by Alan Travis. Pp. 005.

Guardian, (July 12, 2001). *Privatization of the penal system may not be the answer after all: In some cases the public sector's bids have been cheaper and better* by Alan Travis, Pp. 1.17 (UK).

Houston Chronicle, (February 20, 1987). *Bill would allow contracts for private prisons* by Mark Toohey, Pp. 14.

Houston Chronicle, (April 14, 1987). *Clements signs bill on private prison contracts* by Clay Robinson. Pp. 8.

Houston Chronicle, (August 1, 1987). *TDC receives 19 bids to run 4 private prisons* by Frank Klimko. Pp. 17.

Houston Chronicle, (August 19, 1987). *Hearing is planned on private prison.* Pp. 24.

Houston Chronicle, (May 30, 1989). *D.C. inmates protest food at private Texas prison.* Pp. 16.

Houston Chronicle, (September, 15, 1997). *State billing private prisons for hunting, escapees, riot aid.* Pp. 15.

Irish Times, (December 5, 1998). *Private jail industry is booming as crime falls* by Joe Carroll. Pp. 13.

Journal Record, (May 11, 2000). *Prisons filling up with Minor offenders as costs jump* by Ron Jenkins. Pp. 1.

Los Angeles Times, (July 28, 1986). *Proposal for Saugus prison unravels* by Mayerene Barker, Pp. 6.

Los Angeles Times, (June 11, 1988). *1ˢᵗ private state prison planned for Santa Clarita* by Steve Padilla. Pp. 10.

Los Angeles Times, (January 11, 1996). *Firm drops plans to consider Gorman site for prison* by Danica Kirka. Pp. 4.

Los Angeles Times, (April 21, 1998). *Prison firms to merge in $2.9-billion deal* (Reuters), Pp. 16.

Los Angeles Times, (December 18, 1999). *State scraps plans for privately run prison facilities* by Dan Morain. Pp. 35.

Madison Capital Times, (October 21, 1999). *Leasing private prison would cost $24.7 million* by David Callender. Pp. 6a.

Mail on Sunday, (March 17, 2002). *Prison chiefs to build more private jails* by Mark Aitken. Pp. 12.

Milwaukee Journal Sentinel, (December 7, 1997). *Prison in Stanley could mean 350 jobs. Firm proposes building 1,200 bed facility leasing it to state. However, bars use of private prison.* Pp. 5.

Milwaukee Journal Sentinel, (June 16, 1998). *Thompson signs bill ending parole; State lawmaker calls for 3,000 new prison beds to handle inmate increase* by Richard Jones. Pp. 1.

Milwaukee Journal Sentinel, (July 29, 1998). *State awaits ok to send 120 female convicts to West Virginia; Move would mark first time women were shipped out of state to ease crowding* by Richard Jones. Pp. 5.

Milwaukee Journal Sentinel, (October 3, 1998). *State to probe alleged abuse of inmates in Tennessee complains made at prison* by Richard Jones. Pp. 1.

Milwaukee Journal Sentinel, (August 12, 1999). *State inmates in private prison file suit federal lawsuits allege guards tortured, violated civil rights of Wisconsin prisoners in Tenn.* by Richard Jones, Pp. 1.

Milwaukee Journal Sentinel, (June 1, 2001). *Committee backs buying private Stanley prison* by Richard Jones. Pp. 1B.

Milwaukee Journal Sentinel, (October 22, 2001). *Report urges communities to end prison subsidies.* Pp. 9A.

Nashville Banner, (April 21, 1997). *State cooked numbers to make private prisons attractive* by Andy Sher. Pp. A1.

Nashville Banner, (May 12, 1997). *Prison workers get time for privatization gripes* by Andy Sher. Pp. A1.

News Sentinel, (July 16, 1997). *$45 million? Savings estimate given as state eyes private prisons* by Rebecca Ferrar. Pp. A4.

News Sentinel, (November 22, 1998). *Private prison backers adopting new tack* by Tom Humphrey. Pp. G2.

News Sentinel, (August 9, 2000). *Former prison realty CEO set to launch new company to manage technology ideas.* Pp. B4.

Observer, (March 29, 1998). *Hold on a minute* by Nick Cohen. Pp. 30.

Omaha World Herald, (August 6, 1986). *Company hopes to build and run 1st private prison.* Pp. 1.

Omaha World Herald, (September 29, 1998). *Private prison is suggested for those who drink, drive*, Pp. 14.

Omaha World Herald, (May 22, 1998). *Private prison ban vetoed.* Pp. 30.

Orange County Register, (November 28, 1996). *Court to decide on legal immunity of guards at private jails* by Laurie Asseo. Pp. A16.

Palm Beach Post, (February 9, 1997). *Private prisons scoff at Fla. Law* by Charles Elmore, Pp. 1-A.

Pittsburgh Post, (August 3, 1998). *Ohio private prisons.* Pp. A5.

Plain Dealer, (May 25, 1995). *Town profits from prison* by Joe Hallinan, Pp. 5A.

Plain Dealer, (August 25, 1998). *Youngstown inmates' lawyer plans fight against gag order request.* Pp. 2B.

Plain Dealer, (March 11, 1998). *Private prisons or bust.* Pp. 12B.

Press, (August 7, 1998). *Warders step closer to strike after meeting* by Elinore Wellwood. Pp. 3.

Record, (June 15, 1996). *Greater scrutiny at Esmore* by Elizabeth Llorente. Pp. 3.

San Francisco Chronicle, (March 22, 1986). *Private prison has La Honda residents upset* by B. Workman, Pp. 4.

San Francisco Chronicle, (June 3, 1991). *Privatization-old ideas whose time has come/private prison change their image from inhumane to state of the art* by Jonathan Marshall. Pp. A6.

Salt Lake Tribune, (July 21, 1998). *Several states moving toward private and for-profit prisons* by Dan Harried. Pp. A1.

Salt Lake Tribune, (May 7, 1999). *Utah's Wendover willing to bet on private prison Wendover wants private prison to rescue economy* by Brandon Loomis, Pp. D-1.

Santa Fe New Mexican, (July 27, 1996). *Prisons run for profit may turn out not to be all that profitable* by Diana Kim, Pp. A7.

Santa Fe New Mexican, (May 31, 1997). *Johnson already acts like he's on the stump* by Karen Peterson, Pp. A1.

Santa Fe New Mexican, (August 19, 1999). *Brawl fuels debate over private prisons* by Mark Oswald. Pp. A1.

Santa Fe New Mexican, (June 2, 1999). *Cornell a major play in private prisons* by Steve Terrell. Pp. A5.

Santa Fe New Mexican, (February 16, 2000). *Senate approves reopening of vacant state penitentiary* by Bruce Ross. Pp. B3.

Seattle Post - Intelligencer, (December 18, 1998). *Bulging state prisons look to send inmates elsewhere* by Scott Sunde. Pp. A1.

Spokesman Review, (October 10, 1997). *Escapees can be charged, Idaho official says district attorney in Louisiana not so certain* by Betsy Russell. Pp. B1.

Sunday Herald, (January 27, 2002). *Private prison social work plan sees costs soar by 70%* by Alan Crawford. Pp. 2.

Sunday Telegraph, (January 11, 1998). *Straw faces climb down on private prisons* by James Hardy. Pp. 15.

Sunday Times, (December 10, 2000). *Army on standby as prison staff prepare to go on strike* by Neil Mackay. Pp.5.

Sunday Times, (July 23, 2000). *Report on Scotland's first private prison is pulped* by Dean Nelson. Pp. 2.

Tampa Tribune, (December 10, 1996). *Locking in the profits* by Tom Teepen. Pp. 11.

Tampa Tribune, (May 1, 1997). *Prison expert's position questioned* by Margaret Talev. Pp. 6.

The Herald, (March 11, 2000). *Prisoner dies at private jail* by James Freeman. pp. 5.

The Independent, (June 25, 2000). *Analysis: American investors go stir crazy* by James Cruickshank. Pp. 5.

The Independent, (January 12, 2001). *Government will seize control of first private prison* by Ian Burrell. Pp. 6.

The Patriot, (September 3, 1999). *Firm told to stop building jails: Private prisons forbidden in Pennsylvania, Attorney General says* by Peter Durantine. Pp. B04.

The Patriot - News, (April 9, 1987). *Panel says state should continue to prohibit privately run prisons* by Kenn Marshall. Pp. B6.

The Scotsman, (September 14, 1998). *The case for a new defense* by Jenny Booth. Pp. 16.

The Scotsman, (August 13, 2001). *Bars to private prison coming down* by Hamish MacDonell. Pp. 7.

The Times, (May 23, 1993). *Bribery allegations.*

Times-Picayne, (July 17, 1994). *Proud citizens of TV nation* by Shawn McClellan. Pp. T7.

Times-Picayne, (April 14, 2000). *Temporary pact reached on juvenile center: Private prison firm Could regain control* by Steve Ritea. Pp. A2.

Times-Picayne, (April 4, 2002). *House bill changes execution hours: Another keeps away out-of-state prisoners* by Steve Ritea. Pp. A2.

The Plain Dealer, (April 26, 2000). *Union sues on behalf of workers at private prison* by John Caniglia. Pp. 5B.

Tulsa World, (February 16, 1995). *An enforcer for Chicago* by George Will. Pp. N14.

Tulsa World, (March 15, 1995). *State eyes using private prisons* by Barbara Hoberock. Pp. A1.

Tulsa World, (July 19, 1995). *Sale of school land ok'd//Move could lead to prison near Cushing* by Brian Ford. Pp. N7.

Tulsa World, (August 31, 1995). *Prison plan hit on two fronts* by Patti Weaver. Pp. N6.

Tulsa World, (November 4, 1997). *Union attacks use of private prisons* by Barbara Hoberock. Pp. A9.

Tulsa World, (October 18, 1998). *CCA critics point to problems at facilities* by Tim Hoover. Pp. 1.

Tulsa World, (December 9, 1999). *Prison funding sought* by Barbara Hoberock. Pp. 1.

Tulsa World, (July 17, 1999). *Inmate numbers stay above 95%* by Barbara Hoberock. Pp. 14.

Virginian - Pilot, (November 8, 1995). *Currituck takes steps to lure private prison to the county* by Anne Saita. Pp. B2.

Washington Post, (October 10, 1988). *D.C. looks at prisons run for profit: Private facilities may ease crowding* by Saundra Torry. Pp. A1.

Washington Post, (June 13, 1999). *Private prisons: The bottom line* by Ted Strickland, Pp. B1.

Washington Times, (April 19, 1999). *What's Marion Barry up to?* Pp. A18.

Washington Times, (November 16, 2000). *D.C. inmates attack New Mexico prison guards* by Neely Tucker. Pp. B7.

Wisconsin state Journal, (May 7, 1998). *Prison labor contract may be poor risk, state told* by Michael Flaherty. Pp. 4B.

Wisconsin State Journal, (November 12, 1998). *Stories of prison abuse raise concerns; Families call for end to sending inmates out of state after alleged incident in Tennessee* by Alisa LaPolt. Pp. 3C.

Wisconsin State Journal, (September 10, 1999). *Six inmates charged with attacking guard,* Pp. 14-C.

Wisconsin State Journal, (October 9, 1999). *Private prison may still deal with state.* Pp. 3B.

Wisconsin State Journal, (January 29, 2000). *Stanley prison deal won't be easy.* Pp. 4B.

CHAPTER 5

What the Future Holds

The purpose of this book has been to provide a more comprehensive understanding of the contemporary prison and the role played by commercialized incarceration in modern penal operations. Obtaining a more comprehensive understanding of the similarities and differences existing between the sectors contributes substantially to our understanding of the contemporary prison in its many forms. Three specific questions can be answered from the research that comprises the foundation for this book. Each question is presented below in the sequence that its corresponding material appeared in the proceeding chapters.

What similarities and differences exist in the structural and operational characteristics of the public and private prison sectors?

Similar to the public sector, a majority of those incarcerated by the private sector are young, minority males. However, the sectors differ markedly in regard to the custody levels at which inmates are held. For example, a vast majority (9 out of 10) of those inmates incarcerated by the private sector are held at the minimum or medium security levels, whereas only 7 out of 10 inmates held by the public sector are similarly classified. Furthermore, the average number of months served by those inmates incarcerated by the private sector is less than half that served by those incarcerated within publicly operated prisons. Therefore, while the general demographic makeup of each sector's inmates are generally quite similar, their dangerousness (as measured by custody level) and average length of stay differ markedly.

Private prisons are also much less crowded than are publicly operated prisons. In fact, the average public prison operates at or above its designed capacity level, while the average private prison operates well below its designed capacity level. This may be partially due to the private sector's role as a "pop-off mechanism" to house public sector overflow. As the public sector experiences the daily ebb-and-flow of inmates into and out of its prisons, the private sector is primarily used to house those extra inmates that appear especially appropriate for private confinement (the non-serious and the less dangerous offender). Thus, the private sector may have little control over the number of inmates that it consistently houses. Regrettably, this says little about the private sector's desire to maintain or possibly increase its market share. For this, we must rely upon statements made by the private sector that indicate a strong desire to house greater proportions of the total U.S. inmate population.

Penologists have long recognized a correlation between institutional crowding and violence. Since the private sector is less crowded and houses less dangerous offenders, by all accounts it should also experience lower levels of violence. However, findings indicate otherwise. Precisely why the private sector experiences rates of violence that exceed that of the public sector remains unexplained. Perhaps as the court suggests in *Kesler et. al. v. Brazoria County* (1998), private sector violence may be associated to some degree with the quality of its staff. Further explanations may be related to the private sector's relatively high levels of staff and inmate turnover. Each of these factors contributes substantially to an institution's instability by inhibiting the formation of normative and routine behavior. Furthermore, the establishment of inmate leadership, necessary for lower levels of institutional violence, is much less likely to form where relatively short sentences produce a constantly changing environment.

Substantial differences were also found in pay and training where the private sector provided staff with less of each. Reduced levels of pay and training may contribute to lower levels of job satisfaction, an under-prepared staff easily overwhelmed by the prison environment, and a generalized dissatisfaction that can result from comparing one's situation to that of his/her public counterpart. Factors such as these, may directly contribute to staff turnover, institutional instability, and elevated levels of violence.

It is also apparent that there are two separate areas of prison operations that are illuminated by this research - those that a prison's administration have direct control over and can reduce or eliminate in order to maximize profit, and those areas that are more likely to be written into contracts, making reductions or eliminations difficult. For example, the single largest cost associated with prison operations are those related to staff. These are, in fact, the areas where substantial differences were found. The data indicate that the private sector has made aggressive reductions (staff salary and training) in those areas where it is free to do so. Future questions about commodification must specifically examine the effects of privatization upon staff. When considering those areas where adequate data exists, the private sector clearly appears to more closely adhere to a less eligibility ideology than does the public sector. **Current trends suggest that:**

Public sector prisons will continue to retain society's most dangerous offenders. While little apprehension exists in permitting private prisons to house non-violent and low-risk offenders, many public officials are not yet willing to privately house those offenders that pose the greatest risk. Furthermore, questions about potential escapes remain. Until questions about escapes are fully addressed, the danger of housing high-risk inmates in private prisons remains prohibitive. The private sector also shows little interest in incarcerating high-risk inmates. The reason for this disinterest is unknown, but may be partially due to the increased expense associated with high security operations.

High levels of violence will continue to plague the private sector until increases in staff wage and training levels occur. Improvements in these two areas will help attract and retain qualified and dedicated staff that are better able to provide for the orderly operation of its facilities. Furthermore, such a move would decrease the institutional instability generated by high staff turnover.

The typical private prison will seldom exceed its operating capacity. This is due to the private sector's role as a "pop-off mechanism" for the public sector, with its services being needed only when the public system experiences substantial crowding. If crime rates continue to decline or if the popularity of community-based sanctions increase (as some predict), the potential for corresponding reductions in the number of individuals being incarcerated may reduce the number of inmates available for private sector placement.

Concerns about commodification resulting from privatization will persist for a number of reasons. The first of these includes the increased "closed nature" being adopted by the private sector. This approach, gives the appearance that the private sector is attempting to shield its operations from critical evaluation. Such an approach may ultimately cause it more harm than it prevents. Furthermore, if declining crime rates shrink prison populations in the future or if community-based sanctions gain popularity, the private sector may further reduce employee wage, benefits, and training levels to compensate for lost revenue. A failure to provide a more competitive employee benefits package may further fuel the belief that the private employee (performing a public service) is being exploited for commercialized purposes.

What similarities and differences exist in litigation filed against the public and private sectors?

A greater percentage of the lawsuits filed against the private sector allege violations of religious freedoms, due process, cruel and unusual punishments, abuse and harassment, as well as those associated with living and physical conditions. This may indicate a sector that is less developed operationally than is the public sector, has grown more rapidly than it has developed appropriate policy and procedure, or may reflect a sector that is simply less concerned about civil rights issues.

No evidence was found to suggest that privately incarcerated inmates are being hampered from seeking legal redress at a greater frequency than are inmates held by the public sector. Additionally, no evidence has been found to suggest that allegations made against the private sector are more frequently attributable to a pursuit of profit than are those made against the public sector. This determination was based upon a review of those civil rights violations that can be directly linked to financial considerations. These include medical treatment, physical security, and living and physical conditions. In both the medical and physical security categories, the private sector experienced a smaller percentage of suits alleging violations than did the public sector. In the living and physical condition's categories, the private sector experienced a greater percentage of alleged violations. While it is likely that a profit ideology effects the civil rights protections of inmates, based upon these specific factors, no direct link can be established.

Furthermore, a portion of the federal judiciary presents privatization as a rogue form of incarceration having little merit. One court even used the terms "quack" to describe a specific private operator, "commodities" to describe privately incarcerated inmates, and "money-maker" to describe privatization. Terminology of this nature portrays prison privatization as a practice that promotes wholesale commodification and exploitation. These portrayals are given additional credibility when one considers that in about a tenth of these suits, the judiciary compared the private sector to its public counterpart. By comparing private and public operations, and by admonishing the private sector to a greater extent than it did the public sector, the judiciary promotes the position that the public sector has set the absolute standard for prison operations. Regrettably, this perception largely ignores the reality that the public sector has had its share of suits that concern unconstitutional and inhuman practices.

Overall, findings suggest that the private sector more closely adheres to the principle of less eligibility than does the public sector. However, conclusive findings about whether allegations themselves are attributable to attempts at efficiency and profit remain unclear. It is certain, however, that a small but vocal number of federal judges believe privatization to be a practice that places individuals at risk for commodification. Thus, a portion of the federal judiciary clearly perceives privatization as a practice that is more closely aligned with the philosophy of less eligibility than it is with normalization. **Current trends suggest that:**

Suits alleging violations in due process, cruel and unusual punishments, and abuse and harassment will continue to plague private prisons. These alleged violations, in all probability, are due to poor pay, poor training, and high staff turnover. These factors produce a staff more transient and less professional than are those individuals employed by the public sector. A more transient and less professional staff tends to be less aware of legal mandates and constitutional protections than are those that are professionally oriented. Furthermore, the anticipated career-penalties associated with civil rights violations tend to be less motivating for the private employee than are the anticipated penalties for those that view corrections as their profession.

Judicial statements will continue to partially villainize the private sector. These statements may become more prevalent in the future if competition for inmate populations intensify (among private operators and between the public and private sectors) thereby, forcing private operators to consider ways to maintain profit margins. The frequency and overall nature of these statements will be determined largely by the financial effects that competition may have upon the private sector. Greater financial losses will likely result in more frequent civil rights violations and increases in the criticality of judicial assertions.

How is prison privatization being portrayed by the print media?

Findings indicate that prison privatization is portrayed primarily as a financial issue. Issues of profit, savings, and efficiency dominate these portrayals. For example, in over a quarter of those articles reviewed, the subjects of profit, savings, and operational efficiency were presented. Furthermore, in a third of the articles, the sectors were compared with regard to their financial characteristics. These comparisons tended to suggest that the private sector operates more efficiently than does the public sector. The print media also largely ignored the traditional operating ideologies that have historically driven prison operations. The operational objectives of punishment and rehabilitation were mentioned in only one article. By portraying incarceration as a financial issue and not as a practice grounded in punishment and reform ideologies, prisons are generally depicted as human warehouses that are unguided by traditional ideology or reform philosophies. Such a narrow focus tends to suggest that the contemporary prison's only objective is the incapacitation of the offender. Such a presentation promotes the image of the prison as a place without compassion or an interest in inmate reform. The print media's focus on privatization's financial factors displaced a review of substantive information about ideological orientation and quality of confinement. It is certain that only a small portion of the entire privatization portrait is being provided to the citizenry. Such a narrow focus is responsible for producing confusion and speculation about prisons in general, and more specifically about the private prison sector.

Furthermore, the private sector is portrayed by the print media as adhering more closely to the principle of less eligibility than does the public sector. This is apparent in both the language used to describe the private sector as well as in the manner by which financial issues tend to dominate these portrayals. Thus, the portrayal of privatization is often one-dimensional and ignores the similarities and working relationship that exists between the sectors. The print media tends to portray privatization in this manner to a much greater extent than does the judiciary.

Overall, the percentage of titles that portray privatization unfavorably have remained constant since 1986. However, the percentage of titles that portray privatization neutrally have increased while favorable titles have correspondingly decreased. Likewise, the content of the articles themselves have become less neutral and less favorable while the percentage of unfavorable article content has nearly doubled. This suggests that privatization is increasingly being subjected to critical review. These critical reviews may be a contributory factor in the increasingly "closed" posture taken by the private sector. The current sector-wide refusal to disclose information may be interpreted as a defense mechanism intended to stave of further criticism. In fact, the Criminal Justice Institute (long recognized as a leading source of prison related data) reports that the private sector is increasingly hesitant to provide information about its operations. The Institute has, therefore, discontinued its collection of data from the private sector. Since the Institute was the primary source of information on private sector operations, this decision makes it especially difficult for further comparisons to be undertaken.

Current trends suggest that:

The print media will continue to portray privatization largely as a financial issue. Such a portrayal is both easy to create and perpetuate. Furthermore, to many citizens, the issue of privatization hinges solely upon financial issues. Thus, issues pertaining to tax-dollar expenditures are at the forefront of privatization rather than treatment, rehabilitation, and civil rights protections. Societies in general have historically been ambivalent to the fate of their outcasts, so the broader effects of privatization upon offenders and even prison staff will likely fail to garner interest at a level prompting a diversification of media interests.

Portrayals of privatization by the print media will continue to become more neutral and less favorable. As with many criminal justice initiative there exist a "honeymoon" phase. During this phase, hype and unproven speculation persists. Much of this is positive in nature and appears to offer an "easy" solution to a specific problem. In this case, approximately 20 years have now passed during which a more critical and less biased review can be undertaken. Furthermore, a track record has been established upon which comparative analyses have been undertaken. Thus, penologists and various academicians have increasingly begun to challenge many of the benefits long associated with privatization. These challenges effect the prevailing position on this topic. With rare exception, critical review often reduces previously favorable perceptions to those that are more neutral and less favorable. Increased academic review along with the closed posture of the private sector have contributed substantially to decreases in favorable portrayals.

Summary

A few final comments are necessary. First, evidence was found to indicate that private sector staff are currently targets for commodification as evidenced by significantly lower pay and training levels relative to their public counterparts. Lower staff pay and training suggest a secondary commodification of inmate populations. In essence, if a prison can commodify its staff, it can and will commodify inmates.

Furthermore, data suggests that many private sector administrators are former public employees. If the private sector is able to recruit top-level administrators from the public sector, distinctions between the sectors may increasingly diminish. In essence, the ability of the private sector to employ former public employees may erase the uniqueness that once differentiated each sector. It will become increasingly difficult to isolate the effects of a profit ideology upon private sector operations, or to determine where either sector is situated relative to the other upon the ideological continuum.

Due to various legislative acts designed to limit judicial intervention in prison operations, future inmates of both sectors are especially vulnerable to civil rights infringements. In a select number of suits, judicial statements suggested that unconstitutional actions represent a larger, but often hidden occurrence. In essence, if "in-house" grievance processes are being emphasized while judicial participation is simultaneously being de-emphasized, these suits may reflect the types of activity that are pervasive throughout both sectors.

With regard to the media, it is obvious that it has focused primarily upon two separate aspects of the privatization phenomenon: the financial benefits offered by privatization, as well as (and to a much lesser extent) peripheral concerns about its operations. This type of reporting pattern clearly reflects the traditional disregard societies tend to have about the treatment of their outcasts. This ambivalence is currently manifested in the relentless pursuit of efficient and even profitable forms of incarceration.

105

Finally, it is important to recognize that the American prison, whether it is privately or publicly operated is rapidly becoming a closed institution that commodifies both its inmates and staff. Until awareness increases and demands are made to stop this trend, it will continue. While the precise effects of these changes have yet to be determined - suffice it to say that the outcome will, in all probability, not be positive. With regard to privatization, I have said it often and find it fitting to repeat here, "The prison should measure its effectiveness and social value by a diminishing need for its services. Thus, a system that reaps profit from expansion should be approached hesitantly and with a good deal of trepidation."

Discussion Questions

1). Even though private prisons operate primarily at the minimum and medium security levels, they tend to experience assaults at greater levels than does the public sector. Why?

2). If private sector staff are at risk for commodification, how might future staff and correctional institutions be affected?

3). Should students interested in future correctional employment be concerned about the effects of profit and commercialization upon their chosen profession?

Printed in the United States
27945LVS00001B/382-450